THE NILE

The Nile

by Eliot Elisofon

Introduction by Laurens van der Post

The Viking Press
New York

This book is dedicated to my wife Joan, and my daughters Elin and Jill, with the hope that it will help make up for the frequent absences due to a photographer's profession.

Published in 1964 by The Viking Press, Inc.
625 Madison Avenue, New York, N.Y. 10220

Published simultaneously in Canada by
The Macmillan Company of Canada Limited.

Library of Congress catalog card number: 64–11180
Text printed in Holland by N.V. Drukkerij Levisson, The Hague
Photogravure plates by C. J. Bucher, Lucerne, Switzerland

Contents

The figure in brackets at the end of the caption for each
plate indicates the year in which the photograph was made

AUTHOR'S NOTE AND ACKNOWLEDGMENTS

This book, which has taken five visits to Africa and a span of fifteen years to complete, was made possible by a number of overseas assignments for *Life*. In 1947 an assignment to trace the course of the Nile, and to do a photographic essay on the art of ancient Egypt, gave the project its original impetus. I returned to Africa in 1951 to photograph the Ruwenzori range and the surrounding country at the headwaters of the Nile a 1959 assignment, to photograph the places and to recreate the events described by great writers on Africa, afforded another opportunity to visit the Nile basin. And on two other visits — in 1961, en route to Netherlands New Guinea as a member of the Harvard Peabody Museum Expedition, and in 1962, on a round-the-world assignment, again for *Life* — I took the photographs of Egypt that complete the volume.

Valuable assistance was given me during these visits by many people, some of whom I am able to recall here. In 1947: William Snedaeker of *Time-Life* and Sharvarsh Benlian, Arab-speaking assistant, Cairo: in Kenya, Lady Genesta and Lord Claud Hamilton, the Block family, and Donald Ker, one of Africa's great white hunters; in the Sudan Republic, which was Anglo-Egyptian Sudan, British District Commissioners Peter Hogg, A. E. D. Penn, and J. C. N. Donald; archaeologist Peter Shinnie, who conducted me to Meroë; Dr. Nicholas Mallouf, Khartoum; Dr. Hafez Pasha and Abbé Drioton, Cairo. In 1951: Major Van Cools, Superintendent of the Albert National Park; Game Warden Christenson; Henry Godstein, photographer. In 1959: the Thomas Cook Agency, which drew up travel plans that included most of Africa; Henry Reuter, *Life* correspondent in Nairobi; Priya Ramrakha, photographic assistant; Eric Rundgren, white hunter; Game Warden John Savage; Professor Sherry Washburn of Berkeley, California; Harry Stuart Hudson, U.S. Public Affairs Officer in Khartoum; Anwar Galal and Lt. Col. Abdel Fattah Riad, Ministry of Information, Cairo. In 1961 and 1962: Bernard Bothmer, egyptologist of the Brooklyn Museum, who spent many hours patiently guiding me in the plan to correct serious omissions in the field of Egyptian art; the Metropolitan Museum of Art, New York, and the Museum of Fine Arts, Boston, where I was permitted to photograph objects in their collections; in Egypt, members of the Antiquities Department including the Director, Anwar Shukri, and Mustafa Bakri, Moheb Mostafa, and Francis Gatos of his staff: Prince Hassan Hassan and Mohammed Wagdi, Cairo; Francisco Bennett of UNESCO; Dr. J. O. Brew, Director, Peabody Museum, Harvard University; Dr. Edmundo Lassalle.

I owe thanks to the superb technicians of the *Life* photographic laboratory, directed by William J. Sumits, assisted by George Karas and Al Schneider; to Al Assnis, Mauro Rubino, Manya Sweet for developing and printing; to Herbert Orth for color processing. Others of the *Life* staff, past and present, gave generous assistance in various ways: Margaret Sargent, Barbara Brewster, Maureen Walsh, Marge Chapman, Margaret Bassett, Dana Solomon Munro, Margit Varga, Patricia Hunt, Maitland Edey, Josepha Stewart, Charles Tudor, John Dowd, Philip Wooton, George Hunt, and particularly Edward K. Thompson and Bernard Quint.

I am deeply grateful to Caroline Zinsser for aid in research, and to John Lord, J. Kirk Sale, and Jonathan Kilbourn for editorial assistance.

ELIOT ELISOFON

Introduction
by
Laurens van der Post

It has always been strange to me why Africa remained a mystery to the open world for so long. I understand readily that the nations capable of exploration could not discover America sooner because they did not know it was there to discover. Ignorance made it inevitable that they sailed into the New World only by happy accident in their search for a new way to the East. Africa, however, had long been there, inviting investigation in the most provocative manner since it was a mystery not in darkness but in the full light of the sun. Nowhere was the provocation greater and of longer standing than at the Egyptian end of this immense continent. Arnold Toynbee tells us that there in the valley between the First Cataract of the Nile and the Mediterranean a unique society had emerged some four thousand years before Christ and lasted until the fifth century: a span, he stresses, three times longer than that of our own Western society. This ancient Egyptian world owed its life to the river Nile. Once a year the river came down in flood so charged with the rich earth of the interior of Africa that it was almost more gruel than water. As it overflowed the arid desert flats beside its banks it covered them with a film of fertile earth, and as the waters again receded the peasants followed close behind, planting their crops in the mud and even in the shallows themselves. The marvel of it, even for those for whom this ancient society of plenty was a world of bondage, inspired the moving Biblical exhortation: "Cast your bread upon the waters and it will be returned to you after many days, fifty and even seventy-fold."

To this day, though knowledge has dispelled mystery, the wonder of the perennial event remains, and in the war I myself used to feel strangely compelled to go out daily to watch the river water rise under the cloudless diamond skies of the Sudan. The river ran soundlessly, swollen almost level with my eyes, and as I stood there a kind of extra-sensory excitement would grip me fast. Had the flood waters of this river ever failed, Egypt and many races in the far interior beyond its frontiers would have perished. It was serious enough, as sometimes happened, when the annual floods were not up to average. Famine for many then was inevitable. One such famine, as everyone who has read his tales of Joseph will know, lasted seven years. But however much the floods varied, the river itself never quite failed a rainless land. That a society so highly organized as ancient Egypt, so complex, vigorous, creative, and curious about life in all its aspects of mind and matter, did not investigate to the limits of its capacity a river on which it was so utterly dependent is, of course, unthinkable. Indeed, there is evidence of Egypt's concern not only about the Nile which gave it life but about the whole of the Africa out of which the river flowed. For instance, Herodotus records that around the end of the fifth century B.C. the Pharaoh Necho dispatched several ships manned by Phoenician seamen with orders to sail southward from Suez along the coast of Libya (as Africa was then called) for as far as they could go. Three years later they returned by way of the Pillars of Hercules, or Straits of Gibraltar, with the tale that they had sailed for months with the sun rising on their left, until suddenly one day it rose on their right and kept on doing so until they rounded the north of Africa. Herodotus called it "A statement of truth of which I am not convinced myself though others perhaps will believe it."

It is so far as I know the first recorded instance of the acid doubt that soured the return of persons with news of Africa from then on right down to Rebmann, Krapf, Ebhardt, Bruce, and the unfortunate Speke in the nineteenth century. Whether this Phoenician venture, one of the bravest and most imaginative in the history of exploration, was followed up we do not know. What we do know is that efforts to penetrate into the interior of Africa along the banks of the Nile were much more sustained. It is certain that the ancient Egyptians knew the course of the Nile from its delta by the Mediterranean down to Khartoum. The Romans may even have penetrated farther because an expedition sent by the Emperor Nero to follow the Nile into the waste of Nubia returned with the news that their way had been blocked by an impassable swamp — which sounds as if they had reached the Sudd between Malakal and Juba some hundreds of miles beyond Khartoum. Herodotus himself traveled in the fifth century B.C. to the First Cataract at Shellal, and returned to describe Egypt as "the gift of a river." Yet there is no known record of any organized party or single adventurer following the White Nile to its origins, though it was the main stream and only source of life in one of the most frightful deserts on earth. One encounters in the first history only some casual talk of its bubbling up in fountains at the feet of a range of huge mountains in the interior.

However, circumstantial evidence is strong that much more was known about the source of the Blue Nile. It would have been surprising if this had not been so. Lake Tana, its source, lay in Ethiopia, a country in possession not of an African but a Semitic people, claiming kinship with Judah, the most heroic of the twelve tribes of Israel. They had natural and regular contact with the people of the Mediterranean. An envoy of one of the queens of Ethiopia, Candace, witnessed the stoning of St. Stephen, the first Christian martyr, in Palestine soon after the Resurrection of Christ. A persistent legend runs that another queen was the Sheba who visited Solomon in Jerusalem and overwhelmed him with her beauty. Even earlier the Greeks seem to have known about the country and its customs because there is the curious passage in Homer which reports Zeus' absence from Olympus at a critical moment in the affairs of the gods because he had gone to visit Ethiopia, "a land famous for its system of Justice." Considering that Abyssinia to this day has a system of justice not encountered in any other country on earth, this has always seemed to me proof of far more regular and more intimate communication between the nations of the ancient world than our recorded histories allow. But more convincingly still, there is in the same Homer a mention of the Nile as a river which descends "from a cloud hanging over the land of the Ethiopians." Having stood at the source of the Blue Nile myself and walked the highlands around Lake Tana, so high that in the rainy season when I dressed in the mornings I seemed to be combing the thunderclouds out of my hair, I find this an extraordinarily apt and poetically accurate description of the river's origins. In addition I am certain there was a coming and going of all sorts of unknown men with inside information both between Africa and the outer world, and within the continent itself; I believe that this took place on a far greater scale than is suspected and generally considered admissible.

I think indeed one of the main fallacies of the conventional view of this remote past is the assumption that it was a world devoid of intercommunication. We tend in this age of wings to think of the development of intercommunications as pre-eminently our own and to ignore what may have been done by the pedestrians of prehistory. Yet the continent still bears evidence of an ancient traffic and travel that should take all excess out of our assumptions. Even in the far south there are the tall ruins of the city of Zimbabwe and the chain of gold diggings linking it with other ruins down to the Limpopo, and west to the frontiers of Angola. No one knows for certain who built the cities and miners' forts and worked the gold. All we know is that they imply skills and suggest demands of an economy really more akin to those of the Near East and Malabar, and certainly foreign to the races who today occupy the sites. And what are we to make of the rock paintings of south and southwest Africa and their resemblances to those of the Sahara and even to the art of Lascaux, if the great archaeologist, the late Abbé Breuil, is to be believed? And what again are we to say about the figures on smooth South African rock deep in desert and bush painted the Egyptian way, body to the front, heads in profile, men to the neck and then bird or beast above? Again there are the ancient highways of Africa — the footpaths which cut through bush and plain of the continent from south to north, east to west, joining and crossing one another like the lines in the palm of an African hand. I have walked and traveled many of them, including one which comes down the escarpment from Lake Tana, the source of the Blue Nile. It winds down the steep mountain sides to cut unwaveringly through bush, bamboo forest, and plains of grass so high that as I sat on my camel the yellow tassels sometimes brushed my lips, until it joins the Blue Nile again at Roseires in the Sudan. On this same footpath not many years ago I encountered people naked except for garlands of wild flowers, prancing and playing the double pipes of Pan that I have seen portrayed only on Greek urns. I have walked along footpaths in central Africa which the races of Nyasaland assured me led unerringly to the west coast of Africa. They told me also that these were the routes along which the Negro and other native traders of the Atlantic littoral from time immemorial used for their business with the races of Nyasaland and Mozambique. Finally there was the greatest of all footpaths, which provided a route from the Cape to Cairo long before Cecil Rhodes thought of it, and which the races of Africa used in their great displacement from north to south. To this day there is a ford (which must be nameless, since customs and police do not know of its existence) where such an ancient highway crosses the Limpopo River and where one can sit, as I have done, and watch the men who without passports or permits have followed it all the way down from Tanganyika and so cross into the closely guarded and forbidden Union of South Africa. They find work there and in due course, pocketing their wages, return unbeknown the way they have come. If such a traffic still exists today against the competition of motor roads, trains, ships, and airplanes, what must it not have been like when the footpaths had no rivals! So I suspect in the past Africa knew more of these and other African highways than today we can imagine, and along these routes news reached the ancient crossroads of the Continent, at Wadi Halfa and Luxor or the ports of the Red Sea and east coast like Zanzibar, Lama, and Dar es Salaam, and set the bazaars of Egypt and Persia, and market-places of Greece and Rome ringing with their import.

Nevertheless, what is strange to me is how all this knowledge I take for granted was lost except for a few fragments. One of the most meaningful is that recorded by Marinus of Tyre. According to him a Greek merchant, on his way home from India a hundred years or so before Christ, landed on the coast of East Africa somewhere north of the present Dar es Salaam. From there he traveled inland for twenty-five days and arrived in the vicinity of "two great lakes, and the snowy range of mountains in which the Nile has its twin sources." Ptolemy the Great, astronomer and geographer royal, took this story so seriously that when he made his famous map in the second century of our Christian era he showed the Nile dangling from two round lakes watered from a high range of mountains, which he called the Mountains of the Moon. Thereafter the account of this part of

Africa was closed until it was reopened by a German missionary seventeen hundred years later with a report of how he had seen the snows of Kilimanjaro.

The story, contained in the photographs of this book, begins with poetic justice where Ptolemy left off, and I have given so much time to what preceded and surrounded its origins because something of all this remote world and unwritten history seems to me to preside over the focus of the camera which so superbly does the telling.

The story then begins on the Ruwenzori range. Why Ruwenzori? There are, after all, three mountain systems under perpetual snow in Africa with a claim to be the original of the Mountains of the Moon which the Greek of Marinus had in mind. Two of them, Kilimanjaro and Kenya, being nearer to the east coast, are in fact more likely to be the ones he saw than Ruwenzori. But there is something to be said for not depriving any of the three of their association with the moon, because in African imaginations they form a tremendous trinity, though they differ enormously from one another in character and personality. Kenya, the oldest by far, the giant cinder, is always for me the father. Kilimanjaro, the highest of the three, is the son, grown greater than his volcanic forebear. Ruwenzori is the shy virgin daughter and young sister. Kenya has a ring of snow around its twin summits in which it used to wear a diamond of ice with a wonderfully preserved prehistoric buffalo within. The last time I had news of it the diamond was reported to be wearing thin with time and the buffalo had come so close to the air that butterflies were drawn to flutter around it. Kilimanjaro too has a jewel of ice to crown its snow, but with a leopard inside. Only Ruwenzori remains unengaged and wears no ring or seal and still goes veiled, like an oriental virgin, in cloud and vapor which is rarely and then only briefly parted to reveal a flash of secret snow. Therefore to have chosen this most feminine of ranges to represent Ptolemy's Mountains of the Moon seems to me characteristic of Mr. Elisofon's profound feeling for the nature behind appearances in Africa. But, of course, there is another compelling reason why the story should begin with Ruwenzori. Unlike the other members of the trinity, Ruwenzori makes its own direct and considerable contribution to the headwaters of the Nile. In it alone myth and legend, the dream speculation of our first recorded histories, the gossip of centuries, and the sober physical facts that surround the life of the river, meet and are resolved. We begin then among the snows and glaciers, giant flamelike lobelias, huge tree ferns and high heather, scarlet aloes soaring upward like rockets, baroque brachystegia and rococo rain forests, their spiraling trees bearded with druid lichen. It is a scene lifted straight out of the shimmering, burning world of Africa which surrounds it.

Snow may be a commonplace elsewhere in the world but here in Equatorial Africa it is a miracle and so charged with mystery that it is not so much substance as a kind of ectoplasmic glow emanating from the head of the mountain. By day in the mist and the rain below the snow line one moves through rain forests and across mountain heath feeling oneself to be not a climber but a diver finding his way among the tall flickering seaweed, the giant anemones, and all the gothic growths and surrealist shapes of the rough floor of some coral inlet of the Pacific Ocean. And if one is fortunate enough to camp on Ruwenzori on one of its rare clear nights, the scene set against a glow of phantom snow takes on a strange unreal quality as if one were looking on a world of a moon and star botany. The rich, unique, varied plant life is one of the true glories of Ruwenzori. There is no other mountain system in Africa quite like it. Kenya too has tree ferns, giant lobelias, and heather, but it is a bleak and barren mountain by comparison. Where it has a tarn or two, Ruwenzori wears a necklace of lakes. Kenya's speciality is dense bamboo forests and the cedars in whose shade one can sit and watch purple swallows and kingfisher-blue Abyssinian rollers flashing beneath the spreading branches, while far down below toward the Huri hills, the black lava desert and Ethiopian escarpment, Africa burns up its prodigal substance in the sulphur and fire of the sun. But above the tree line Kenya is a harsh authoritarian mountain with a field of ice in its miter so that the Swiss guides of the man who first climbed it called it the Diamond Glacier. Kilimanjaro's main fascination for me is the great primeval forest which encircles it from where the grass, which is pressed against it like silk by the wind from the Masai plains below, comes to a sudden end, to where the forest and ice begin. It is a dense, deep, dark, fairy-tale forest beloved of wrinkled elephant, colobuses with black fur coats and white cravats, leopards, dappled with sullen gold and lacquer black, gallant bushbuck and filigree dik-dik with ears like petals of saffron cannas. But beyond the tree line, this great round head of a mountain is Cromwellian and terribly austere. Only Ruwenzori has bamboo and forest in plenty, and yet behind her veil of cloud and vapor is constantly giving of herself in plants, flowers, and trees, and feeding lakes and rivers in the thirsty land below with endless streams of amber water.

And all that I have had so say about Ruwenzori in so many words is established by a shot of this remarkable camera. With rare economy, a single chord of photography gives us all that is essential of Ruwenzori in the orchestration in this four-thousand-mile journey of a river from the secret heart of Africa to the sea, and so on into our desperate twentieth-century day. Just one shot is enough to represent Ruwenzori's contribution to the Nile: a view of the Semliki River which has all the rivers of Africa in legend and history within it, and immediately becomes an image of the continent as it was before men set eyes upon it.

From there Mr. Elisofon turns with inspired logic to the mountains of the Mufumbiro range. In this range are the active volcanoes of Africa, and they are of the greatest importance to the story. The ice, snow, and rain which fall on the mountains may supply the waters of the Nile, but the fires that still burn in the Mufumbiro range made the great reservoirs like Victoria, Albert, and Edward and supplied the beds which contain them. They are the last of the volcanic forces which created the Great Rift in the earth of Africa, and indeed not only in Africa, because this great divide runs right through Abyssinia, the Red Sea, Jordan, Syria, central Asia, and on into Siberia, and is sealed at either end by two lakes that are twins in shape, Baikal and Tanganyika. This is an older world by far than the one we left behind on Ruwenzori. As we look through the eye of this sensitive camera, across some of the tallest and most remarkable euphorbia candelabra trees standing with a strange consecrated air as if they had been lifted straight out of some Byzantine cathedral in Constantinople, and contemplate the bare fire-seared mountain tops, a sense of the antiquity of Africa is evoked that is poignant and immense. One can begin to believe that Africa, as some geologists claim, once really was part of an immense continent which included Madagascar, the Deccan of India, and Australia. Considering how slowly water nibbles the land and remembering the great oceans that now separate the fragments of the vanished continent, one has some inkling of how old Africa is. Even the name that the geologists gave this super-continent — Gondwanaland — for me always has a strange "Gone-with-the-wind" ring.

It seems right too that in this Mufumbiro range should live one of the earliest and most human of anthropoids — the gorilla. I have never forgotten my first glimpse of gorillas, on the slopes of Mount Mikeno: a group of seven adults and three young coming out of the forest to a clearing by a stream. The day was clear. Though the forest was as dense as any I had ever seen, it was yet filled with a starboard-green light so intense that the coats of the gorillas themselves were not black but looked as if damp and shade had made verdigris of their hair. There was nothing ferocious about them. Indeed, I was immediately struck by their demonstrative affection for one another. At one moment two of them embraced and seemed to kiss. But the climax for me came when they reached the water. I had fully expected them to go down on all fours to drink directly from the stream with their mouths as other animals do. But they sat down upright on their haunches, fastidiously cleared the surface of the water with their hands, and then scooped it up to their lips. That slight gesture seemed to set them a million and one years apart from the hundreds of other glittering animals species that I know and love, and to bring them strangely close to man. I crouched there with my guide watching them until they went back into the forest, and as they vanished an extraordinary feeling of desolation and bereavement came over me. All this may seem irrelevant, because there are no gorillas in Mr. Elisofon's story, but for me it is important to relate this incident because it is this kind of Africa which is implicit and unerringly evoked for me in the photographs of Ruwenzori, Semliki River, and the Mufumbiro range.

From there this dynamic camera moves quickly down the mountains to the prodigious lakes that suckle the young Nile, and soon we stand at what is generally regarded as the source of the Nile itself — the Ripon Falls. The choice of this spot as the beginning of the river has never satisfied everyone. Indeed, the connoisseurs of Africa have disputed it hotly and would like to have it placed hundreds of miles south, where rises the most remote tributary of a tributary of the Kagera River which flows into Lake Victoria and itself has its origin in the mountains of Tanganyika. Others find this discrimination between the rivers and lakes that feed the Nile invidious and prefer to talk of the "sources" of the Nile rather than the "source," and the plaque which marks the spot where Speke, the first known European to have reached it, stood seems to support this view for it reads: "Speke discovered this source of the Nile on the 28 July 1862." The photograph which shows this plaque is of historic importance because both the plaque and the Ripon Falls (which Speke named after the President of the Royal Geographical Society of his day) are now forever under water as a result of the Owens Falls Dam and hydroelectric scheme farther downstream. Speke for many reasons has always touched my imagination more than any other of the Nile explorers. It seems that he more than any of the others had the courage of his intuitions. It was a remarkable piece of perception that brought him to the Ripon Falls, and he reported his discovery to London in such terms of explorers's authenticity that they are to me poetic. "The Nile," he cabled London, "is settled." The weariness, illness, danger, and suffering of more than two years of searching, and the whole truth of his desperate mission seemed to demand at the moment of discovery that it should be reported in no other way. It all has a striking parallel in our own day. The terms in which Edmund Hillary announced to John Hunt, the leader of the first successful Mount Everest expedition, that he and Sherpa Tensing had reached the summit were of the same breed and scorched temper. Hillary's phrase, "We've done her, the bitch" (a remark not officially released at the time), was, I am certain, spoken in the same tone in which Speke would have told Lord Ripon and Murchison, had he met them around a far bend on the river, that the Nile had been "settled."

From the Ripon Falls we follow both the Albert and the White Nile into the plains of northern Uganda and the southern Sudan. By now one has all possible confidence in Mr. Elisofon's camera to portray the physical scene. But can he do the same for the complex animal and human life which now appears on the banks of the river? He does not fail us, and avoids the traps into which so many cameramen in Africa fall. For instance, one of the main blights of African photography is an obsession with the physically great and horrific, coupled with a tendency to poke fun at the animals of the continent, which is the only characteristic that somewhat spoils some of the Disney nature documentaries for me. In this process not only the animal itself but also the immense riches, the wonder and significance of what is small and delicate in Africa, pass almost unnoticed. Mr. Elisofon does not ignore the great but dismisses the horrific — that is, the abnormal — while he honors the small. He has telling shots of birds, not many because the theme is long and complex and has to be stated with economy and discipline if it is ultimately to be rendered with clarity, but enough to show that they are one of the great neglected glories of Africa. In this part of Africa the waters are an astonishing sight at dawn and dusk. I have seen the sky of a cataclysmic sunset so crowded with birds, and the waters below already so full, that the urgent weaving flights instinctively stacked themselves and queued up in the pink zones of the air as aircraft do when waiting their turn to land at our crowded international airports. By day there are flights of birds so dense that the first time I saw them in the distance I took them to be smoke of bush and veld fires fluttered by the whirling eddies of the melting quicksilver noon. Mr. Elisofon even honors the insects in this record, and there is one shot of a swarm of locusts that could serve as an illustration of the plague which was dispatched to punish Pharaoh for breaking his promise to Moses. One of the greatest hunters of Africa told me as a boy, "Africa is God's country, cousin, but remember always it is Old, not New Testament country." Mr. Elisofon clearly has grasped this point. But perhaps the two outstanding examples of his excellence at interpreting animals are his shots of elephant and zebra. In both of these he has somehow succeeded in depicting the quintessential animal. With the elephant he expresses what is for me its extraordinary and profound relationship with time. The elephant belongs to time, is a child of time, in a way that no other form of animal life is. We humans increasingly make an enemy of time; but for the elephant time is its wayside hospice, and accordingly it lives longer than any other animal, takes longer to conceive, and is born rich with history. I have seen a baby elephant immediately after its birth in the bush in Africa and already, with its corrugated brow and marble skin, it looked older than any centenarian I have ever known. It is antique from birth, and life only makes it more antique. And this is how the camera sees the elephants: drenched in time as deeply as that ancient Africa which is stretched out along the river banks with its face turned to the sun.

The zebra is a different and perhaps more complex story. It is extraordinary how the native peoples of Africa themselves vary in their attitudes to the zebra. Some tribes abhor it, some will eat it, others will not, and can even feel so violently about it that I have seen one African who was with me on an expedition vomit at the mere suggestion, though the other bearers of a different tribe were doing so avidly. A few Africans see in its vivid bands of black and white an image of fullness and completion. Once an illiterate African chief said to me, "We black and white in Africa are like the zebra: it does not matter whether the arrow pierces it in a black or a white part, the animal dies just the same." But there is no doubt that to all the zebra is most decorative, a child of effortless eurhythmic movement nursed in vast plains on great distances with speed of flight as its chief defense. And this is how it is depicted here in one of the finest photographs of zebra that I know.

We come next to the Sudd, one of the great marshes of the world. The Nile, which has hitherto collected its tributaries from the mountains and cut its path down to the plains with such speed and purpose, here seems to lose the will and the way to the sea. It meanders through hundreds of square miles in uncertain streamlets and lazy lagoons among dense papyrus growths, against hyacinth barriers and around termite mounds pointed at the sky like rocket-launching pads. A passage had to be hacked through the papyrus before steamers could ply the river between Uganda and the Sudan, and the cutting back of hyacinths and papyrus has to be kept up constantly if it is to stay open. It used to be the most abhorred part of the river, and I knew many old Sudan hands who drank more beer and whisky to help them over the monotony of the Sudd than on any other section of the journey. Yet to me the Sudd was always of an unusual and entrancing beauty. The sky overhead might be burning with destruction but deep in the cool shades of the elegant and tasseled papyrus stalks one could see birds, animals, and flowers rarely, if ever, to be seen anywhere else, such as the gleaming gray shoebill, the sensitive setatunga or Mrs. Grey's waterbuck, water lilies like sacred temple flowers, and giant blue and purple convolvulus. Once when the fires of the Nilotic tribes who live in and around these marshes had set the papyrus alight — and it is astonishing how fiercely so wet a water-plant will burn — I saw the flames driving all the secret life of the swamp either into the water or into the air. There was a moment at one bottleneck in the channel where the flames came very close and the water around us was turned into a goulash of crocodiles, snakes, rats, mice, scorpions, and so on, while the smoke, the locusts, and other insects escaping from the flames brought a twilight to the sky which was illuminated only by scarlet bee-eaters, so vivid that they looked like scraps torn from the flames themselves as they dived and darted in and out swiftly among the hapless insects to gorge as they had never gorged before.

When the sun goes down over the Sudd, from islands and shallow earth suddenly the bluest of smoke will rise to merge with the blue of the night as the tribes one by one light their fires under the green leaves and growths that they accumulate hard by their cattle camps. They do this to protect the cattle, whom they love more than life itself, against the mosquitoes that emerge from the swamp at nightfall. The tall herdsmen will stand in the smoke by their charges all night long, resting like herons on one leg at a time, the other drawn up and the foot pressed against the knee of the one in use, their hands clasping a long throwing-spear dug firmly into the earth. All around them the night will vibrate with the high pagan bagpipe music of mosquitoes marauding in such vast hordes that outside the shelter of smoke or net I have myself sometimes been near panic because of a feeling that they have left life with no air to breathe. Yet under cover of my net I have found it an exciting sound and marveled how the stars themselves seemed to respond and tap out their music.

As for the people themselves, they were when I knew them and I believe still are largely enclosed in an extremely remote context of time. Their cattle, in whose being almost mystically they participate and in whose sounds they hear the voices and read the wishes of their remote ancestors, are one of the oldest breeds on earth, a breed which testifies to this prehistoric intercommunication in Africa of which I have spoken. I have seen the same humped-back cattle with their immense spread of horn in the keeping of Hottentots, Batawana, and Heroro on the shores of Lake Ngami, in the Kalahari desert, and the edges of the Okovango swamps some four thousand miles away in southern Africa. The legends, stories, customs, and strange yet real sense of honor and chivalry of these peoples have an odd Homeric quality, and they themselves, particularly in some of their cattle rituals, reminded me of the descriptions of the assorted peoples who allied themselves with the Trojans in the war waged on the great plain of the *Iliad*. Mr. Elisofon again does not fail to render their archaic quality.

One of the most interesting things about the history of this part of the world is how the English came to love this marshland so unlike their own gentle and civilized land, and what passionate protagonists they became of Nilotic tribes as utterly remote from themselves as Dinka, Nuer, and Shilluk. In fact the Sudan administration divided spontaneously into two distinct classes of men, northerners and southerners, the northerners ardently devoted to the Arabic-speaking races and believing them superior to all others; the southerners passionately attached to the Nilotics, seeing them as noble pagans cruelly exploited in the past by the Arab world and determined to defend them and their ancient spirit not only against the northerners but against their own civilization as well. The southerners, with that genius the English have for understatement, never called the Sudd by its name but always spoke of it affectionately as "the Bog." Some of the finest disinterested work ever done by the English was done in this part of the world, and even today when they have gone it is well worth while taking with one on this journey down the Nile some of the many books which deal with the lives of the officials, the humble forgotten district commissioners well known all over Africa, the simple, straightforward soldiers and dedicated rangers who identified themselves with the peoples of the Sudd, such as "Fergie (Ferguson) Bey" or Wyndham's "The Gentle Savage."

What is perhaps even more remarkable is that for all the passionate differences of interest between northerners and southerners, the British administration in Khartoum, to which Mr. Elisofon soon takes us, never took sides but quietly blended and transcended both in a vision of the Sudan as a whole. This was possible only because in many ways the Sudan under the British was the nearest thing to a Platonic government that the world has ever seen. They themselves had no settlers in the land as they had elsewhere in Africa. They had only some seventeen hundred young men schooled in the humanities at universities, a band of doctors, veterinary officers, and soldiers seconded from the army, to run the vast land. They had, I believe, no other temptation than that of governing well and with honor. The result was that when I knew the Sudan the peoples seemed to me free of the negations and the crippling complexes and paralytic resentments one used to find in most other parts of the great empires of the West. The change in atmosphere, even after Egypt, was immense, and as I stepped out of the river steamer at Wadi Halfa to board the train for Khartoum my spirit always felt unburdened by the frank, direct, free, uncomplicated way in which the Sudanese looked me straight in the eye when I spoke to them. There was a phrase in common use in the Sudan in those days which expressed all this better than I can do it. I would talk to my Sudanese soldiers and camel men and sooner or later they would say, "Yes, that was before the government came" or "that was after the government came." The "coming of the government," of course, was the moment when the British finally took over the Sudan in 1898, and the phrase in the way they uttered it was invariably charged with the relief and gratitude that they still felt over an event which marked their deliverance from the chaos and horror of their inarticulate and random past.

I myself experienced a most moving demonstration of what the Sudanese felt about the coming of orderly and incorruptible government. In the war I was sent from Roseires in the Sudan into Abyssinia to steal behind the Italian lines with an immense camel train loaded with guns, ammunition, money, and other supplies for the revolt we were organizing against the Latin invaders. I was promised that at the foot of the formidable Ethiopian escarpment the Abyssinian partisans would have mule trains gathered to take over the loads from my camels and transport them into the mountains beyond. I had the strictest orders that my camels, and above all my camel men, who were all civilians from Kordofan, should not be taken into the mountain areas or on any account into our battle zone. When I arrived at the foot of the escarpment there were no mules of any sort, only a desperate plea from the front for the arms and supplies that I was carrying. I called together the sheiks in charge of the various camel trains around me and frankly explained the situation to them, telling them that I had no power or authority to compel them to go on with me but that unless they and their camels went with me into the mountains we might well lose the war against the Italians. The prospect of going on and up into the mountains clearly shocked them, and after a long and passionate discussion an old sheik from El Obeid rose and addressed us all to this effect: "My feet are covered with blisters, my body with sores. I am hungry and exhausted and my clothes are torn to rags. I have nothing to warm me against the cold and rain in the mountains. But I am old enough to remember what the Sudan was like before the government came and if the government would wish me to go on with my camels I shall go on." That won the day and we went on, camels and all, not only into the hills but on into the forward battle area.

Now these very people in all their multitudinous variety are represented in this picture story just as their past and present made them, just as I remember them in all their manliness, and as their independent future beckons them from the Sudd to that great crossroad of history on the Nile, Wadi Halfa. And there I will leave them.

The journey to the sea is only half done, but henceforth the pictures move into the world of recorded history which is in the main familiar to most. About it I would say only this: the many-sidedness of Mr. Elisofon's great visual gifts are as evident here as in the less sophisticated and complicated life of the river. Africa not geographically but within the meaning of its preponderant nature and spirit is well behind us. The land before us is only technically part of Africa. In essence it belongs body and soul to the ancient Mediterranean world, particularly the Middle Eastern and Levantine part of it. Yet the touch with which the camera searches it out and spreads it open for our view is as sure as ever. In particular the photography of the temples of Abu Simbel, Luxor, the Thebes of Tiresias and Oedipus, the statues, the painting, the mummies, the tombs, the Pyramids, and the Sphinx, seems to me to achieve the summit of what a camera can do. This will not surprise those who know Mr. Elisofon's book on African sculpture. He has not gone into this great venture just by instinct and spontaneous combustion of purpose, but has served the exacting apprenticeship without which no art or skill is possible. He has served it so well and in this book achieved so much that I feel he is now an honorary African, and I wish there were an institution to confer on him the "freedom of the dark continent" just because of the light he sheds upon this great river end of it.

Finally, there is another reason why I find Mr. Elisofon's work important. For many centuries there has been no African painting to represent this continent visually to the world. Africa, of course, is constantly being painted, but the idiom is not African. The European painters who come to Africa see it only with European eyes. Many of them do this because they are not capable of ridding themselves of their European conditioning. As many, I believe, do so because they recoil, un-consciously, from the African scene, afraid, perhaps, of the implications of what they see: the violence of light and shade under a sun which destroys as much as it creates; the powerful and uninhibited color, aboriginality of shape, and unfamiliarity of form spread out with such prodigal abundance before them. D. H. Lawrence's presumption — so strange an error in one with such an intuitive understanding of the nature of the physical world — that Africa is "the continent of dark negation" may well be theirs as well. And even should they know, as we who are of Africa know, that all the gentleness and delicacy of color and being that they are accustomed to in their neat, ordered, garden civilizations are to be found too in the brief African evening and dawn twilight hours when the night and life forgive the day for what it has done, how could they render it, since it is so swiftly all enveloped in darkness? Easier by far to paint it in the colors and conventions to which they are accustomed — just as it is easier and more comfortable to judge us Africans as if we were just another version of themselves. Sadly, too, these painters have imposed their kind of painting on the African painters. They have done this so easily because I believe that, in painting, what is a liberation and enlargement of the range of the senses of one generation declines very easily into a tyranny for the next. What we see throws a more immediate spell over our imaginations and senses than what we say and write. This I think partly accounts for the violence with which some painters have had to reject traditions hitherto dear to them in order to break through into a way of their own, as, for instance, Van Gogh had to do. Naturally the African-born painter is dominated by the European example. From the moment he is born he sees nothing but painting in the European tradition. Reproductions of the European masters are constantly being thrust on his attention, and when he comes to train for his art he does so in a European school under teachers from Europe. Long before he sets out to paint on his own his African painter's soul is lost in a hypnotic European outlook. Even in my native South Africa, where the European has lived now more than three hundred years, his native visual sense remains bound to the conventions and fashions of Europe, perhaps even more so today than a century ago. I myself feel this lack of visual representation of Africa so much that sometimes I find myself as a writer slipping into a painter's role and trying to do with words what still has to be done by brush and canvas. But the time is coming quickly when the European scales will drop from our eyes and we shall take up again the dazzling vision, recover the dynamic rhythm, and recapture the swift darting movement where the rock painters of Africa left off. Until then only the camera which is free of the tyranny of the painter, as is Mr. Elisofon's, can fill the vacuum and point the way to liberation of our visual African senses.

Opposite (fold out) :

MAP OF THE NILE
by Rafael Palacios

A detail from this map appears at the head of each chapter.

THE NILE

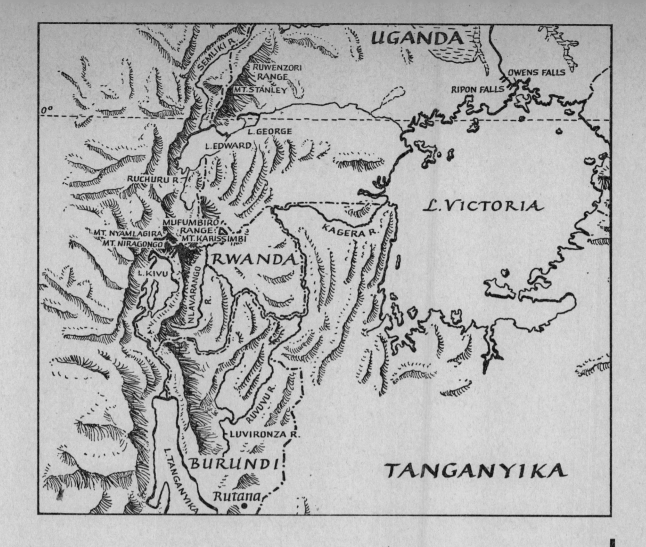

I
The Headwaters:
Fire and Ice

The Nile River — the longest, most vital, most self-sufficient, most varied, and most powerful river in the world. From its headwaters deep in the mountains of central Africa to its delta on the shores of the Mediterranean, it stretches some 4160 miles and describes an arc of thirty-five degrees, one tenth of the earth's north-south circumference. Its basin covers more than 1,100,000 square miles, an area one tenth the size of Africa and one third the size of the United States, and encompasses everything from volcanic mountains to desert, from swamps to thunderous falls and rocky rapids. Upon its waters and its annual floods approximately forty million people (in Egypt, the Sudan, and Uganda) depend for their very existence, while another ten million people (in Ethiopia, Kenya, Tanganyika, the Congo, Rwanda, and Burundi) feel its indirect effects. So mighty are its sources that after its immense journey across the desert, where it loses almost half its water through evaporation, it still gushes into the sea at the rate of 420,000 cubic feet per second (roughly 1,000,000,000 gallons an hour).

The Nile begins in the rills and rivulets on the high mountains of western Uganda and northern Rwanda, where clouds bearing moisture from the South Atlantic hover continually. From these mountains the headwaters flow into the lake systems of Uganda until they meet at Lake Albert, on the country's western border, and form the beginning of the White Nile. The White Nile then sweeps briskly into the Sudan until it is choked in the vast 50,000-square-mile swamp known as the Sudd, but eventually breaks free and continues down to Khartoum. There it meets the Blue Nile, coming down from Lake Tana, some 5800 feet above sea level, high in the Ethiopian mountains. Together the two Niles pour out of Khartoum, are met by the Atbara, the river's only major tributary, and then cut through a series of six deep cataracts, or rapids, for about a thousand miles until they reach Aswan. Then the Nile rolls slowly across the Egyptian desert in a long straight line all the way to

Cairo, at the apex of the vast Delta. After spreading through the 4600-square-mile Delta region, it finally pours out into the Mediterranean.

The origins of the Nile River have fascinated men for at least twenty-five hundred years. Herodotus in the fifth century B.C. wrote of a bottomless "abysmal" lake from which the waters came; Aeschylus held that Egypt was "nurtured by the snow" of inland mountains; Aristotle mentioned a "silver mountain" at the Nile's head. In the second century A.D. the Alexandrian astrologer, mathematican, and geographer Ptolemy, on the basis of reports from Arab travelers, drew an amazingly accurate map of the Nile showing its origins in two lakes rising in what he called the Lunae Montes — the Mountains of the Moon. But it remained for the nineteenth century to discover the real headwaters and for the twentieth century to map them accurately.

Today geographers trace the origins of the White Nile to two separate water systems high in the central African mountain ranges that were formed when the Great Rift cut down through Africa in the early Tertiary period. One is the Victoria system, described in the next chapter, which gathers its waters from the eastern slopes of the Mufumbiro mountains, sends them through the Luvironza River into the Kagera River, from which they finally flow into the huge Lake Victoria; Lake Victoria, in turn, empties the waters into the Victoria Nile, which flows through Lake Kyoga, over the magnificent Murchison Falls, and finally into Lake Albert.

The second system is the Albertine system, a spectacular combination of towering peaks, turbulent streams, deep lakes, and meandering rivers that covers some 16,000 square miles. It has its headwaters in two short but lofty mountain ranges, the Ruwenzori and the Mufumbiro, from which the water pours in torrents into two small but vital lakes, Lake Edward and Lake George. The slow-moving Semliki River then carries the water from Lake Edward northward to Lake Albert, where it joins the Victoria Nile and begins its long journey to the sea as the White Nile.

The Ruwenzori are perhaps the most impressive mountains in Africa, even though they are no more than sixty miles long and at most thirty miles wide. They are located just north of the Equator — with their eastern slopes in Uganda and their western slopes in the Congo — in a part of Africa that is still remote and relatively uninhabited. Their peaks are covered most of the year with heavy, low-hanging clouds, but when the clouds lift the snow-topped mountains shine and glitter as though they were indeed made of silver, as Aristotle imagined.

Six of the Ruwenzori mountains are over 14,500 feet high, and each of these is named for one of the early explorers of central Africa: Emin, Gessi, Speke, Stanley, Baker, and di Savoia. It is fitting that Mount Stanley, which crests at 16,794 feet, should be named for the famous journalist-explorer Henry Stanley, who first sighted the Ruwenzori during an expedition of 1887-89; it was one of his aides (a man appropriately named Lieutenant Stairs) who first climbed up them to the 10,000-foot mark. Later expeditions explored the lower reaches, but it was not until a British Museum expedition of 1935 that the main peaks were accurately mapped. Even today, scores of valleys are still unexplored, and dozens of peaks over 12,000 feet high are still unnamed, unclimbed, and unmapped.

The Ruwenzori area is one of the wettest parts of the earth, with approximately three hundred and sixty days and two hundred inches of rain each year. For the people of the lower Nile this is an extremely fortunate meteorological accident, for it is this continual flow of water from the Ruwenzori slopes that feeds the Nile all year long, even when the Blue Nile and the Atbara River, whose waters come from the seasonal monsoon clouds in Ethiopia, have dried almost to a trickle.

The Ruwenzori are broadly classified as a "mountain forest" region, but there are actually six separate areas of vegetation, ranging from tropical through temperate to alpine. Up to about 6500 feet — the upper limit for human habitation — is the *grass zone,* consisting of foothills covered with tall elephant grass and acacia trees. From 6500 feet to 8500 feet is the *forest zone,* where most of the mountain game — bushbuck, wild pigs, monkeys, lions, and several species of cat — are found. From 8500 feet to 10,000 feet is the dense, dark *bamboo zone,* with stalks of bamboo sometimes as high as fifty feet and as much as three feet in diameter at their base. The next region — from 10,000 feet to 12,500 feet — is the beautiful *tree heath zone,* the largest heath in the world, where giant trees drip with heavy, water-soaked lichens, and mosses and deep sphagnum beds cover the ground. From 12,500 feet to 14,000 feet is the *zone of lobelias and senecios,* two tropical trees which are the fascinating African versions of familiar American plants: the senecio (or tree groundsel), a broad-leafed plant sometimes twenty feet high and eight inches thick, with four-foot high flowers, is a cousin of the common aster; while the lobelia (or flower-candle), a man-high, narrow-leafed tree with stalks of yellow, pink, and blue flowers, is a relative of the common American lobelia. Under these plants stretch miles of mosses and lichens, some of which take on riotous green, yellow, and orange colors. The last region, above the 14,000-foot snow line, is the *snow zone,* where permanent glaciers sprawl between bare rock.

Where the Ruwenzori waters begin with snow and ice, the streams that roll down from the second great mountain range of the Albertine system, the Mufumbiro, begin with fire. At least five of the mountains are active (though so far harmless) volcanoes, and heavy, low clouds condense over their red-hot lava flows. The range, which rises in northern Burundi seventy miles south of the Equator, cuts at right angles across the north-south line of the Great Rift Valley, and its clouds thus provide water for two different rivers: streams from its southern slopes pour into the Congo system, and streams from its northern and northeastern slopes feed the Nile.

The Mufumbiro range is just a little larger than the Ruwenzori, about eighty miles long and thirty-five miles wide. Its highest peak is Mount Karissimbi, an extinct volcano, at 14,865 feet. Several other mountains are more than 12,000 feet high, among which both Niragongo and Nyamlagira are active volcanoes. On the slopes of Mount Mikeno, now extinct, lives a large and protected colony of gorillas, usually harmless and fearful of humans, but ferocious when attacked or when protecting their young. Also on its slopes is the tomb of Carl Akeley, the famous American photographer-naturalist who pioneered in the establishment of African game reserves (especially the Albert National Park in the nearby Congo) and who is thought to be the only man ever to strangle a leopard with his bare hands.

Waters from the Mufumbiro's northern slopes run into a series of streams that eventually form into the Ruchuru River, which gushes its way for forty miles through low foothills and shallow gorges until it pours into Lake Edward. This lake, which also drains the smaller Lake George, is some 3000 feet above sea level and forms the meeting ground for the Mufumbiro and Ruwenzori waters before they descend to Lake Albert at 2030 feet. Located just two miles south of the Equator, Lake Edward is about forty-four miles long, 365 feet deep, and in places as much as thirty-two miles wide; including the large Dweru Bay at its northeastern end, it covers an area of 820 square miles.

Lake Edward (named by Stanley in 1888-89 for the future Edward VII) is both beautiful and of practical use. Its beauty comes from the thick, soft haze that overhangs the water during the dry season and from the small geysers and tiny crater lakes — one of which has deep purple waters — around its edges. Its usefulness comes from its fish — mudfish, perch, tiger-fish — which the Africans catch in great numbers, fish being a cheap source of protein, a necessity in this area where the natives are prevented from killing game. Uganda has increased its fish production from ten thousand to seventy thousand tons over the last dozen years and now produces about $6,500,000-worth a year.

At the northern end of Lake Edward the water runs out into the Semliki River, a 150-mile stretch of slow-moving currents that sweeps out into the Congo, cuts back eastward to form the Congo-Uganda border, and finally drops down to Lake Albert. Though short, the Semliki is extremely colorful, with almost every variety of African game living in its grassy basin — elephants, rhinoceros, lions, hippopotamuses, buck, and impalas — and almost every kind of water bird hovering above its marshy shores.

The Semliki ends its short life at the southern end of Lake Albert, the long, 1640-square-mile lake that marks the end of the Albertine system. Here the mountain waters flow northward through the lake for almost a hundred miles before they reach the companion waters of the Victoria Nile, mix with them in swirling eddies, and finally roll out together as the Albert Nile, now only 3600 miles from its final destination.

Plates

23

The Margherita glacier on the slopes of Mount Stanley in the Ruwenzori range. Mount Margherita, at the tip of Mount Stanley, is the third highest summit in all of Africa and the thirty-sixth highest in the world. An Italian, the Duke of Abruzzi, made the first ascent in 1906. Today the Margherita can be climbed with relative ease by a well-equipped party. [1951]

24-25

The zone of lobelias and senecios, just below the snow line in the Ruwenzori. The broad-leafed plant in the left foreground is a senecio, while the narrow-leafed plants in the right foreground are lobelias. The ground is covered with several colorful varieties of moss, including the sphagnum, which holds huge amounts of water in deep beds that sometimes sink five feet or more. [1951]

26

Black Lake, one of a series of small lakes strung like silver shields between the Ruwenzori peaks. In the left foreground are mature senecio plants, at the beginning of the zone of lobelias and senecios, which show the characteristic accumulation of dead leaves along the trunk. In the immediate foreground are low immortelles, related to the immortelle plants of the Swiss Alps. [1951]

27

Mount Stanley in the background, with its Alexandra peak (16,313 feet) on the far left. The mountain is seen from an elevation of 13,250 feet, near the "Camp of Bottles," where climbers are supposed to leave their names on a piece of paper in a bottle. Heavy clouds normally put an impenetrable blanket around the mountains, but during certain seasons of the year the peaks are occasionally visible. [1951]

28-29

The dense Ruwenzori heath at about 10,000 feet, showing the characteristic twisted trees, whose trunks are sometimes three feet in diameter. The dripping lichens which hang from the branches — resembling the "Spanish moss" of the southern United States — absorb water from the continual rains. Delicate pink ground orchids deep in beds of sphagnum can sometimes be seen from the crude trail. [1951]

30

Water from the cloud-covered upper zones of the Ruwenzori runs off the mountains in thousands of rills; eventually the rills grow into rivulets and the rivulets into streams like the one shown here, which pour down the western slopes of the Ruwenzori into the Semliki River, emptying eventually into Lake Albert. The largest of such streams are the Mubuku and the Bujubu. [1951]

31

Inside the crater of Nyamlagira, one of the active volcanoes of the Mufumbiro range in northern Rwanda. The formations in the foreground are hardened lava flows, while in the middle distance smoke can be seen rising from still-active vents. [1951]

32-33

The Mufumbiro plains, with Mount Niragongo, which has erupted recently, on the far left, and Mount Mikeno, now extinct, on the right. The plains are covered with a variety of temperate and tropical flowers, such as the yellow daisies in the foreground. The large cactus-like trees are euphorbias, now very rare. [1951]

34

Marshes along the Semliki River, in the foreground, with Lake Edward in the background. An elephant browses near a group of white pelicans. The green grass and low acacia trees are typical of the open park lands of the central African plateau. This area of western Uganda is one of the two sections of Africa where big game — elephants, giraffes, rhinoceros, buck, lions, and leopards — is still found in great numbers. [1951]

35

Two male hippopotamuses fighting over a female in the Ruchuru River, which flows into Lake Edward. The formidable mouth span (three to four feet) and the protruding eyes and ears can be clearly seen in the hippo on the left. So sharp are the hippo's tusks — really two long incisors in the lower jaw — that one of the animals was able to punch holes in the bottom of a steel boat used by the early explorer, Samuel Baker. [1951]

36-37

The Semliki River, in the foreground, leaving Lake Edward on its northward journey to Lake Albert. The view is from Ishango Bluff. Among the waterfowl of Lake Edward are ducks, geese, cranes, storks, fish eagles, and kingfishers; shown here are white pelicans and cormorants who feed on the numerous fish of the lake. By day a cloud of small flies hangs over the water. [1951]

38

African fishermen on Lake Edward with their day's catch of mudfish and a variety of perch. Many of the fishing boats on the lake are simple dugout canoes, like the one being poled on the far right, but an increasing number are modern power-driven boats, like the other two shown in the picture. These fish will probably be cleaned and dried at one of two modern processing plants nearby. [1951]

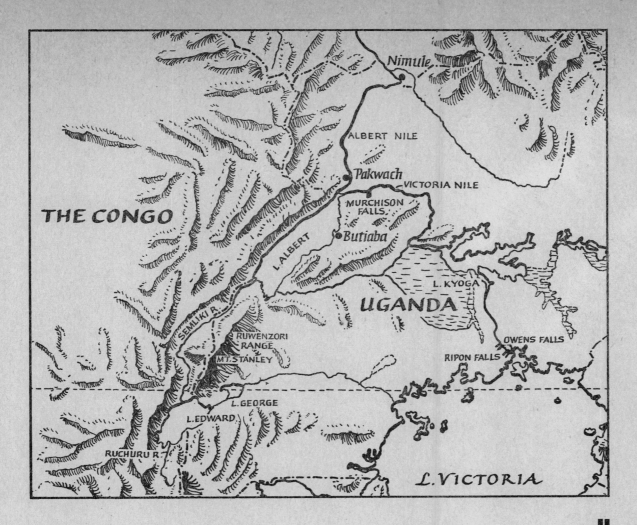

II
The
Victoria Nile

Near the Rutova Mission, a peaceful-looking cluster of buildings at Rutana in the new nation of Burundi, squats a pyramid of stones. It was set there in 1938 in memory of "all those who, ever since the ancient Egyptians, have searched for the sources of the Nile." Among those commemorated is the Englishman John Hanning Speke, whose exploratory passion brought him — after years of frustration and privation — to a triumphant sight. On July 28, 1862, standing on a slight rise of ground, some hundreds of miles northeast of Rutana, he watched the waters of the Nile emerge from the northern end of Lake Victoria in a gliding curtain thirteen feet high, across a chasm 1310 feet wide, which he at once named Ripon Falls in honor of the president of the Royal Geographical Society that had financed his expedition.

The pyramid at Rutana stands beside the first source of the Victoria system, the Luvironza River, which descends from foothills in northern Burundi to the Ruvuvu River and then joins the Nlavarongo to form the mighty Kagera River. This river, which flows first west and then back east, drops more than 2000 feet in 429 miles before it empties into Lake Victoria in the middle of its western shores. There it mingles with the other waters of this 26,000-square-mile lake until it finally flows out at the northern end, where Speke saw it emerge.

But the spot where Speke stood is now well under water, inundated in 1954 by the water backing up from the huge Owens Falls Dam built a mile downstream from Ripon Falls, which is now also submerged. Since the construction of this dam, Lake Victoria has become the largest reservoir in the world: it remains the largest fresh-water lake in the Eastern Hemisphere and the second largest in the world. It also gives the Nile its first title. The green waters of the Kagera leave Victoria by way of the dam to form the Victoria Nile. Contemplating the rock-lined area immediately below Ripon Falls in 1907, Winston Spencer Churchill noted: "It is possible that nowhere else in the world could so enormous a mass of water be held up by so little masonry." With the completion of the Owens Falls Dam forty-seven years later, when he was Great Britain's Prime Minister, Churchill saw his vision turned into reality. The ten 15,000-kilowatt generators at Owens Falls now supply the major part of Uganda's power needs.

Less than a century ago, Uganda had no such grand structures. Although the area was strongly and ably ruled by five well-organized tribes — the Baganda, the Banyoro, the Batoro, the Banyankore, and Basoga — it still had hardly been touched by outsiders. The tribal political systems, though primitive by European standards, had courts, procedures of justice, codes of chivalry, and even well-functioning parliaments with prime ministers and cabinets; but their economic systems were still crude and undeveloped.

All this began to change when Speke and other Europeans entered what is now Uganda in the mid-nineteenth century and began to impose their rule. By 1894, after a series of pacts with the local chieftains, Britain finally established a protectorate over the heart of Uganda and two years later took control of the entire country. During the sixty-six years of its reign Britain did a great deal to build up the colony economically, fostering a solid agriculture based on cotton, coffee, and tea, and to prepare it for eventual independence.

That independence finally came on October 9, 1962, when Uganda, with a population of some six and a half millions, formally attained its nationhood as an independent member of the British Commonwealth and the one hundred and tenth member of the United Nations. Now the Ugandans are at work building the country's economic power, using their natural resources — such as the power of the Nile and its Owens Falls Dam — to move the nation into the modern world. Foreign capital and technical assistance are helping to improve its agriculture, while overseas businesses and African entrepreneurs are strengthening its industries. Although seventy per cent of the people are still illiterate, the new country is greatly expanding its educational program, and its Makerere College, one of the finest in Africa, is turning out a steady stream of qualified men.

Like Gaul, Lake Victoria is divided into three parts. Its southern half lies in Tanganyika; its northern half, partly in Uganda and partly in Kenya. Surrounding the lake, especially to the north, is a land of immense color and excitement. Churchill wrote of the landscape, in his *My African Journey* (London, 1908):

"I had travelled through tropical forests in Cuba and India, and had often before admired their enchanting, yet sinister, luxuriance. But the forests of Uganda, for magnificence, for variety of form and colour, for profusion of brilliant life — plant, bird, insect, reptile, beast — for the vast scale and awful fecundity of the natural processes that are beheld at work, eclipsed, and indeed effaced, all previous impressions. One becomes, not without a secret sense of aversion, the spectator of an intense convulsion of life and death. Reproduction and decay are locked struggling in infinite embraces. In this glittering Equatorial slum huge trees jostle one another for room to live; slender growths stretch — as it seems in agony — towards the sunlight and life. The soil bursts with irrepressible vegetations. Every victor, trampling on the rotting mould of exterminated antagonists, soars aloft only to encounter another host of aerial rivals, to be burdened with masses of parasitic foliage, smothered in the glorious blossoms of creepers, laced and bound and interwoven with interminable tangles of vines and trailers. Birds are as bright as butterflies; butterflies are as big as birds."

And through this landscape around Lake Victoria roams the world's largest concentration of game. Both the heavy forests and the less cluttered plains provide succulent pastures for numerous varieties of animals — antelope, zebras, elephants, giraffes, and the more truculent herbivores such as rhinoceros and buffalo. The area thus provides prolific hunting grounds for lions and leopards and for their followers, the scavenger hyenas. As late as the mid-1940s it was not unusual for planes to fly at a very low altitude over the upper Nile valley so that the pilots and passengers could watch huge herds of game galloping away from the aircraft's shadows, which often startled even the hippopotamuses from their wallows.

There was a wholesale massacre of game in many parts of Africa during the latter part of World

War II, however, and for some time thereafter. The animals were killed for three reasons: to check the sleeping sickness spread by the tsetse flies that followed the herds, to furnish food, and to provide farming land for an increasing population. Strict laws had to be passed to protect many species.

At one time elephants seemed in the greatest need of such protection. Apart from their value as a prodigious supply of meat for the natives — who killed them with spears, with poisoned arrows, and by trapping them — the ivory in the elephants' tusks attracted poachers, both amateur and professional. An African bull elephant stands eleven feet high at the shoulders and carries a pair of tusks weighing up to a hundred pounds each that curve out more than ten feet from his upper jaw. Herds of more than a hundred elephants can still be seen on the Nile's banks, specked by the brown tick birds that feed on the parasitic insects which infest the herds, and followed by white egrets, the cattle birds common throughout Africa. Though elephants are slow breeders (their gestation period lasts between eighteen and twenty-two months, and usually only one calf is born at a time), their numbers are now increasing.

The African elephant is being saved from extinction not only as a result of the watchfulness of game wardens but also because the main target of the poachers has shifted. The increasing value of the African rhino's two nasal horns now makes it a more profitable trophy. These horns — actually concretions of hair — are highly prized in Arabia for the manufacture of dagger hafts whose magic properties are supposed to protect their owners in moments of peril. The horns are also sought after throughout the Far East for their reputed qualities as an aphrodisiac. The rhinoceros has always offered one of the finest of trophies to the hunter, especially the square-mouthed, so-called white rhino, whose habitat is the lush savannah east and north of the Albert Nile (that section of the Nile in northwest Uganda from Lake Albert to the Sudanese border). Actually light gray in color, the white rhino differs from the more common black variety in size (it is bigger), in shape (its head is more massive, its neck humped), and in diet (it eats only grass). In 1910, Theodore Roosevelt, that formidable collector of big game, shot five white rhinos in Uganda for exhibit in three museums he was laboring to fill with heads and horns.

Roosevelt's journal of his 1909-10 safari reads like a catalogue of wildlife. From his camp by the upper Nile, he noted buffalo, waterbuck, monitor lizards, cormorants, flycatchers, elephants, leopards, white ants and driver ants, fish eagles, hartebeests, eagle owls, bushbuck, lions, bats, hippos, and crocodiles. The section of the "young" Nile along which Roosevelt was hunting is noted for its concentration of crocodiles in particular. Churchill too had reported this and suggested a reason for it. At this point the Nile is a swift stream carrying an accumulation of dead fish and animals that are appetizing to crocodiles, which do not eat fresh food but stow away prey until it has reached a state of putrefaction. From the Owens Falls Dam downstream from Lake Victoria, the Nile flows north with the urgency of a young river. Forty miles of its three-hundred-mile course between Lake Victoria and Lake Albert are rapids, and so the Victoria Nile is not navigable. As it flows toward Lake Albert, it passes through Lake Kyoga, discovered in 1874 by Charles Chaillé-Long, an American who was chief of staff under Maj. Gen. Charles George (Chinese) Gordon, ruler of the Sudan for the Khedive of Egypt. The Victoria Nile enters Lake Kyoga by a southern arm and at once loses much of its force in a swamp of papyrus, water lilies, and miscellaneous growths. It leaves the lake by Kyoga's most westerly arm and almost at once reassumes the characteristics of a river in torrential course.

Cutting into the rock, the Victoria Nile forms two waterfalls between Lake Kyoga and Lake Albert: the Karuma Falls and the Murchison Falls. The latter is generally considered to be the most impressive spectacle provided by nature on the Nile's long journey to the sea. The river races through a funnel of rock twenty feet wide and spills out in two separate arms that thunder down about a hundred and thirty feet to explode on the rocks below.

The Victoria Nile feeds Lake Albert at its northern end and there mingles with the waters of the Semliki River, which flows into the southern tip of the lake from its sources in Lake Edward. When the Nile leaves Lake Albert it becomes the Albert Nile. The combined strength of the Victoria Nile from the southeast and the Semliki from the southwest provides the Albert Nile with the sixteen per cent of flow that is its contribution to the great Nile which streams through Egypt to the sea. The Nile that emerges from Lake Albert is some two thousand feet above sea level and does not fall appreciably until it reaches the southernmost border of the Republic of the Sudan near Nimule.

Traveling on the Albert Nile is like making a voyage into the past. The stern-wheelers that ply leisurely between Butiaba on Lake Albert and Pakwach on the river were brought to Uganda part by part from England early in this century. Of shallow, four-foot draft, they lurch occasionally when they strike a hippopotamus suckling its young on the river bed. Their upper decks, screened against insects, provide cabins for the well-to-do. It is not uncommon to see a pool of fresh blood at the waterline, a sign that Moslem passengers have killed a goat for supper. There may be one or two native hunters aboard, their bows and arrows slung, offering for sale baby monkeys — tiny quivering balls of fur with their heads pressed against their bellies.

Life is not easy for the Africans of this region. At some time in the remote past, the Hamites, the Caucasian chief native race of North Africa, began to migrate to the south. They met Negroes moving northward from central and southern Africa, clashed with them, and ultimately intermarried. The resulting mixture produced the peoples now called the Nilotes, a proud race that has tended to stand aloof from the material benefits of Western civilization.

The Nilotes' attachment to their primitive culture is deep-rooted, and their afflictions are numerous. Diseases that have been checked elsewhere are still common among them; in addition, two particularly dread diseases — sleeping sickness and bilharziasis — are rife. The former is transmitted by the bite of tsetse flies, which seek shade and therefore infest the acacia trees that afford pleasant meeting places for the villagers. Bilharziasis, a disease of the blood, is caused by a parasitic flatworm that enters the body through the agency of a minute fresh-water snail native to the Albert Nile and carried thence down river. It is bilharziasis that produces the lassitude often observed among the Nilotic peoples.

The valley of the Albert Nile is broad and swampy, confined on either side by gentle slopes. Its character does not change very much as it enters the Republic of the Sudan just south of Nimule, although within the space of little more than four hundred miles the river is twice renamed. It is called the Bahr el Jebel, or River of the Mountain, when it enters the Sudd — the swamp region of the southern Sudan — and the White Nile (Bahr el Abyad), when it is joined by the Bahr el Ghazal (River of the Gazelle), flowing from the west, at Lake No. (Some authorities prefer to consider the Bahr el Jebel merely a section of the White Nile.) When it leaves Uganda the Nile has traveled nine hundred miles from its most remote headstream in Burundi and fallen some four thousand feet. In its journey, it has begun to lose the appearance of youth and to take on a look of middle age.

Plates

45

The plaque commemorating Speke's first sight of the Nile leaving Lake Victoria, with the eddies from Ripon Falls in the background. The plaque reads: "Speke discovered this source of the Nile on the 28 July 1862." Both marker and falls are now submerged beneath water backing up from the Owens Falls Dam, a mile farther downstream.
[1947]

Below, right: The Owens Falls Dam, looking southward toward Lake Victoria. The typical open park land and rolling hills of Uganda seen in the background are now transected by huge steel power lines running from the dam's generators throughout much of the new nation. [1959]

46-47

An aerial view of Lake Kyoga, in central Uganda, which resembles an amoeba with long, meandering arms. The banks of the lake are heavy swamps of reeds that cut much of the Nile's force as it comes rolling in from Lake Victoria. [1959]

48

The Victoria Nile between Lake Kyoga and Lake Albert, its surface rippled by heavy raindrops. Floating with the current are small green plants called "water cabbages," as well as clumps of grassy earth. The water here is about twenty feet deep and lazily placid, but it will soon be rushing over two deep falls farther downstream.
[1947]

49

The Murchison Falls, on the Victoria Nile some twenty-four miles from Lake Albert, are the river's single most spectacular sight. The falls were discovered by Sir Samuel Baker in 1864 and named by him for Sir Roderick Murchison, a British geologist who was a founder of the Royal Geographical Society. [1959]

50-51

A group of zebra running across open grasslands at sunset. Though their oddly striped hides make excellent camouflage in the tall grass, they are continually on the lookout for lions, their chief enemies. They usually travel in large bands, sometimes of more than a hundred. [1959]

52

An adult crowned crane, one of the most beautiful birds of central Africa. These birds generally live in small bands, feed in the open on herbage and small animals such as frogs, and sleep at night in trees. Some African tribes consider it bad luck to kill these cranes. [1947]

53

Vultures in the Murchison Falls Reserve feeding on the body of a dead elephant killed by poachers. Vultures and hyenas are the two most active scavengers of the African plains and together have been known to finish off an entire elephant. [1959]

54-55

A herd of elephants on a sandy plot, with acacia trees in the background, to the east of Lake Victoria. They use their trunks to spray sandy earth over their backs, in order to drive away the flies. [1959]

56

A large crocodile slithering into the Victoria Nile. Sometimes twenty feet long, these reptilian monsters are not uncommon along this stretch of the river, where they feed both on fish and on mammals washed away and killed by the rapids. Crocodiles, using their giant tails to stun their victims, have been known to seize animals or even men who come too close to the bank. [1947]

57

A young girl of the Madi, one of the principal tribes settled north of Lake Albert along the Albert Nile. The scarification of her upper body, made in infancy by rubbing dirt into open cuts, is typical of the Madi, who favor large triangular welts on the torso and thick, vertical scars along the forehead and arms. [1947]

58-59

The Albert Nile on its way northward from Lake Albert, a thin sliver of light in a darkening landscape. The fringe on the bottom edge of the river is made up of large acacia trees, and the banks themselves are cluttered but well-defined swamps. [1959]

60

A Madi mother with her child at a camp on the Albert Nile. The woven basket in which the child is resting can be strapped to the mother's back for easy carrying when they are traveling. The young girl on the right is wearing a simple garment of manioc leaves suspended from her waist in front and back. [1947]

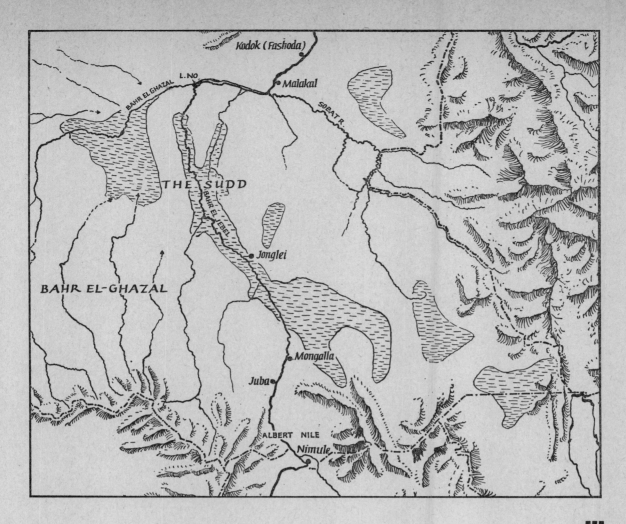

III
The Sudd

Nudity is now forbidden in the Republic of the Sudan. But in the Sudd the law is more honored in the breach than in the observance, for its inhabitants are among the most independent people on earth. Tenacious of their ancient culture, the Nilotic tribes of the Sudd resent attempts by the distant — and to them somewhat alien — government at Khartoum to change their way of life. Moreover, the law banning nudity is difficult if not impossible to enforce, since the Sudd is an area where travel is arduous at best. The people of the Sudd live in twenty-five thousand square miles of swampland, much of which lies under water for the greater part of the year.

As a geographical feature, the Sudd is unique — a kind of landlocked Sargasso Sea. It is a labyrinth of tiny lakes, channels, and lagoons, none of them solidly defined, since their banks are composed of islands and archipelagoes of mud and shifting weeds. Here it is as though the Nile were a rope frayed in the middle, the solid bulk teased and parted into a hundred strands. For in the Sudd the river loses its cohesion and its force.

At the point where it enters the Sudan, the river still retains some of the vigor of its youth. It cuts through the granite outcrops of the last mountains it encounters on its way to the sea (spurs of the highlands that form the Congo-Nile watershed), seethes through a chain of rapids, and just north of Nimule tumbles down a series of little falls. By the time they reach the level plain, the waters of the Nile have traveled a thousand miles from Burundi. But here the river loses half its power, since for every gallon of water that flows into the Sudd, another gallon is dissipated.

The Arabs used to call the area the Barrier, because it blocked their way to the rich slaving grounds and ivory preserves of East Africa. For centuries it helped keep the source of the Nile one of the world's greatest geographical secrets. It blocked the determined explorations of two centurions sent on an expedition up the Nile by the Emperor Nero around 66 A.D. More than eighteen hundred years later it trapped Romolo Gessi (the gallant Italian explorer of Lake Albert who had been one of Chinese Gordon's lieutenants) for three terrifying months. Gessi was returning to Khartoum in 1881 from a tour of duty as governor of the southern Sudan. Most of his escort of four hundred men died of starvation or fever before they could force their way out of the Sudd, and Gessi himself only lived long enough to reach Egypt.

The first permanent channel was hacked through the Sudd in 1899; for years that channel remained only six yards wide. Even today constant efforts must be made to keep a passage open. The sides of every steamer passing through the Sudd are deliberately rammed against edges of the channel to keep its banks firm. The present width of the channel is forty to fifty yards, but already a new hazard has appeared in it: proliferating water hyacinths, which may well result in impeding traffic anew if the problem they present is not soon solved.

On each side of the permanent channel through the Sudd — and sometimes far into the swampy horizon — wave the fronds of the papyrus from whose pith the Egyptians made their paper. The plants grow fourteen feet tall, their color changing from pale green near their roots to a darker green as they reach their full height. Beside them soar thickets of elephant grass, its stems as stiff as bamboo, and clumps of ambatch, each spike of which is as thick as a man's wrist and bears blue convolvulus flowers. In the swamps at the base of the plants spread water lilies and mosses. From time to time a block of *sudd* (Arabic for floating vegetable matter) breaks off from the mass of plants and floats away slowly until it reaches an obstruction. There it stays for a while, perhaps forming an "island" of its own and fortified by the river silt drifting in among its tangled roots, until the whole pattern of channels and islands in the area begins changing again.

The islands of vegetable matter that make up the comparatively solid part of the Sudd support a good deal of life. Elephants can move on some of them, though they do not frequent the area. On the Sudd's borders live lions and leopards. There are many antelope, including the Mrs. Grey waterbuck, a species so rare that a license to shoot a specimen is issued to a man only once in his lifetime. Hippos and reptiles, particularly crocodiles and giant lizards are plentiful. There are birds of many kinds, the rarest of them the strange silver-gray shoebill. There are giant herons, kingfishers, cormorants, Nile geese, goatsuckers, and hawks. But of all the forms of life in the Sudd by far the most multitudinous are the insects, chief among them mosquitoes, tsetse flies, and white ants. The last — which are really not ants, but termites closely allied to roaches — have a curious habit of either undermining or covering everything they wish to consume. Their settlements are marked with conical heaps of iron-hard earth that rise as high as twelve feet. The white ants will eat anything but metals and poisonous minerals. Yet the people of the Sudd consider them a delicacy, to be fried in their own fat and eaten like popcorn.

The strange customs of the Nilotic tribes have occasioned some historic misconceptions. Early travelers, catching sight of Dinka tribesmen in their classic stance (holding a long staff, with one foot resting on the knee of the other leg or pressed up against the small of the back), returned to medieval Europe with stories of a race of one-legged men, the Monopodes. Authors of medieval bestiaries recorded the existence in Africa of a strange beast, first reported some centuries earlier by Pliny: an animal with one horn pointed to the front and another to the rear. Called the "yale," it was later incorporated in the Beaufort family coat of arms and eventually into that of the Royal House of Windsor. The yale was — and is — simply an ordinary Dinka cow. Dinka tribesmen still twist the horns of their cattle into unnatural shapes, as they did in Pliny's time.

Down river from the Uganda border in the Sudd live the six principal tribes of the southern Sudan — the Dinka, Nuer, Shilluk, Lur, Madi, and Bari. They are the peoples for whom the Sudan is named, after the Arabic Bilâd-es-Sudan, or Land of the Blacks. The first three tribes are the inhabitants of the swamps. They number about 1,300,000. A product of mixed Negro and Caucasian blood, they are a handsome dark brown and tend to be tall and slender. They are herdsmen and shepherds by calling, polytheists, and free men by disposition. The Dinka refused to recognize the authority of the central government until 1928.

The Shilluk, Nuer, and Dinka are alike in their regard for their cattle, around which the tribes' spiritual as well as physical lives center. The Nuer communicate with the ghosts of their ancestors by rubbing their animals' backs. A tribesman may be named after the form and color of his favorite beast; his wife after a cow she milks. Cattle, rather than currency, provide the medium of exhange, and are used to pay fines or buy brides. (A young Nuer beauty is normally valued at twenty or thirty cows.) Cattle are sometimes sacrificed, but only at the most important ceremonies. Their milk makes cheese, the more pungent for being mixed with their urine to curdle it. Blood is drawn from the necks of cattle by spear cuts, congealed, either baked or boiled, and then added to a porridge of millet. The tribesmen find uses even for their cattle's dung. Wet, it serves as a plaster for walls and floors. Dry, it provides fuel. The ashes from the burned dung are used as a cosmetic powder or tooth cleanser, or dampened and applied to the hair to stiffen it into formal shapes and dye it a reddish orange.

Both men and women bear scarifications formed by incisions made with a small iron knife during various initiation ceremonies. Dirt is rubbed into the resulting wounds. The traditional patterns serve for tribal identification as well as for ornament. Every Shilluk girl bears a series of keloids formed like a string of beads over her brows. Men of the Dinka and Nuer tribes have a number of fine horizontal lines cut across their foreheads. Among some tribes, the lower incisors of young boys and girls are removed. One reason for these practices is to test the stoicism of youth about to be accepted into adult society.

Existence is obviously no easier for the Nilotes of this region than for those who live along the Albert Nile. Not only are the diseases and natural hazards prevalent in the Sudd many indeed, but the tribesmen's economic structure produces no real wealth. They are nomads rather than farmers. Yet they are tenacious of life, and their social structure still reflects tribal practices that developed during the childhood of mankind. The present-day rulers of the Shilluk may be compared with the kings of antiquity, for like the priest-kings of the early Greeks they are at once potentates and potential sacrifices — or were until 1959, when the government at Khartoum passed a law making the slaying of a tribal ruler a capital crime.

To the Shilluk people their *reth* (king) was traditionally a rainmaker, and if his power to produce rain failed, or his term as sovereign reached its end, he was sacrificed. Even today the reth is surrounded by ceremony and mystery. After his coronation he retires for three days to a sacred mound called the *aturwic,* surmounted by walls woven of millet straw. During this period no one, not even his favorite wives or his sons, may look directly into his face. Commoners must crouch before him, twisting their heads back over their right shoulders. It is a custom that has changed as little over the years as the Sudd itself.

The country of the Nuer, Shilluk, and Dinka extends along the river from Mongalla, approximately a hundred miles south of Uganda, to Malakal, about three hundred miles north as the shoebill flies but a lot longer by the Nile's tortuous course through the Sudd region. It takes three days for paddle-steamers to negotiate the river from their starting point at Juba (just north of Mongalla) to the clear water above Malakal — about four hundred and eighty miles, or the length of the river Seine. When it emerges from the swamps, the Nile has traveled a third of its way to the sea.

Half the Nile's waters have been lost among the roots and suckers of water plants in the surrounding swamps. The Bahr el Ghazal has joined it from the west and the Bahr el Zeraf (River of the Giraffe) from the south, but neither has had an appreciable effect on the Nile's flow. Now, however, its strength is restored. Just south of Malakal there enters from the Ethiopian hills to the east the powerful Sobat, replenishing all that has been soaked up by the Sudd and restoring to the Nile its breadth and majesty.

The river has left the vast primitive wilderness of the Sudd behind and begins to encounter towns with a recorded history. The first of importance is Kodok (formerly Fashoda), site of a clash between Great Britain and France during the race by great European powers to carve out imperial empires in Africa. The only relic that remains of what was once a major international crisis is a small tablet set into the wall of the police post there, reading simply: "Marchand, 1898."

The tablet commemorates the incredible feat of Capt. Jean Baptiste Marchand, an intrepid soldier-explorer, in marching three thousand miles across mid-Africa and occupying Fashoda in 1898. At the time, the British were busy trying to reassert the authority of the Khedive of Egypt in other sections of the Sudan, where a fanatical Moslem sect had seized power. Marchand's occupation of Fashoda had only symbolic value for the French, since he had only a few hundred men in his command, while the British had armies in Khartoum and Omdurman to the north as well as gunboats on the Nile. The British, under Gen. Horatio Herbert Kitchener, could have wiped out Marchand and his men with ease. The danger lay in the possibility that any military action between the groups might lead to a major war between the two nations in Europe. Feelings ran high in both countries, but eventually reason prevailed, and the governments in Paris and London divided Africa into spheres of influence. Marchand (who fought as a French general in World War I and did not die until 1934) was finally ordered to withdraw.

The British were left in control — either directly or indirectly — of almost the entire length of the Nile, and their mark still remains on it.

Plates

67

A young man of the Nuer tribe in the Sudd region of southern Sudan. He has covered his body with ash from burned cow dung and is training his hair with a helmet of cow dung and its ashes.

[1947]

68

Thick beds of papyrus growing on the banks of the Nile as it flows through the Sudd. Another stream of the multi-channeled river can be seen on the other side of these beds. [1947]

69

The S.W. (stern-wheeler) *Melik,* cutting its way south from Malakal to Juba through the Sudd,

pulling freight barges at its side. About a hundred feet long and drawing from three and a half to four feet of water, such steamers are the principal means of transportation along most of the Nile.

[1947]

70-71

Top left: A Nuer cow whose owner has twisted its horns, one forward and one back, in a shape as personal as a signature. *Top right:* Shilluk houses in Malakal, on the Nile at the northern end of the Sudd. The most common dress of the Shilluk is a short Roman-style toga, seen in the man on the right, and almost everyone carries a walking stick. *Bottom:* Shilluk cattle grazing on the meager grass along the banks of the Nile near Malakal. [All 1947]

72

A Nuer tribesman relaxes in a typical pose, one leg drawn up like a stork, with a hand-carved paddle for balance. The dugout canoe behind him is used for fishing, which is often done with a barbed spear.   [1947]

72-73

A Shilluk brandishing his spear during a war dance at a celebration near Malakal. The dancers carry heavy crocodile-hide shields, heavy clubs, and spears, and all wear elaborate headdresses, made of fur, feathers, or even old felt hats. [1947]

74-75

Above: A horn made from a kudu antler and a gourd is used by a Shilluk tribesman to summon his neighbors to a funeral. Both the men and women of the tribe are tall and slender and wear a great deal of jewelry. *Below:* Elders of a Shilluk village listening to a woman (in the center of the circle) on trial: Her daughter has run away from her husband, and the mother refuses to make her go back. Like most African tribes, the Shilluk have an intricate code of marriage behavior. [Both 1947]

76

Three photographs of a Shilluk ceremony to purify a village after lightning has struck and burned the high roof of a hut. *Top:* First, a small goat is sacrificed (center foreground), its belly cut open, and bits of its entrails thrown into the ruined hut. Two men with long poles knock down the parts of the wall still standing. *Center:* Next, the villagers — men, women, and children — carry away the pieces. *Bottom:* Finally, after all the pieces are collected in an orderly pile well outside the village, the village is considered purified, and a new hut can be started.   [All 1947]

77

Top: Anei Kyr, the *reth* (king) of the Shilluk, wearing a white cotton toga tied with a piece of silk, a European beret, two bracelets made from an elephant's tusk, and a necklace of ostrich egg shells. Behind him is the *aturwic,* the mound to which he retires after the coronation. *Bottom:* A group of Shilluk men averting their faces as the reth walks by, a custom observed by intimates and commoners alike. The hut behind them has the typical pointed roof of millet thatching and air holes instead of windows.   [Both 1947]

78

A young Shilluk girl wearing a necklace of aluminum from a plane wrecked in the area, engraved with a large nail by a local artist. In addition to the scarification welts, her forehead is decorated with two strands of ordinary white buttons and several bands of commercial beads.   [1947]

79

A Dinka sub-chief near Malakal, with his toga-like dress and the typical thin, horizontal lines of scarification on his forehead.   [1947]

80-81

A peaceful river scene at Kodok (formerly Fashoda), on the Nile north of the Sudd. The Nile, now regaining its settled course, can be seen in the background, above the line of trees. [1947]

82

A young Nuer tribesman with six horizontal scarification bands on his forehead. In the rite marking their initiation into adulthood, the Nuer boys' foreheads are cut to the bone; few cry out, though many lose consciousness afterward. [1947]

74

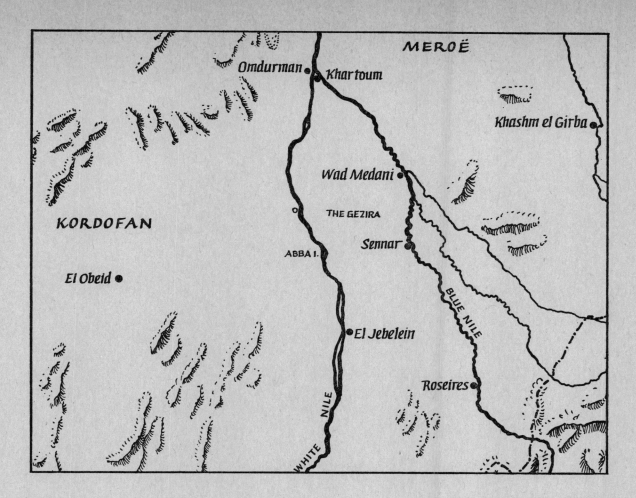

IV
The Spear and the Crescent

Omdurman, now the Sudan's largest city, lies on the west bank of the Nile, across the river from the Sudanese capital, Khartoum. In the spectacular splendor of the desert dawn the Moslem inhabitants of Omdurman daily make their devotions. Above them, against a riotous sky, gleams a symbol that is a permanent reminder of a triumphant past and a militant faith. Visible from every point of the sprawling metropolis, it is the broad stabbing spear of the Sudan joined to the crescent of Islam, the personal emblem of the Mahdi (divine guide), over whose tomb it glitters.

When the man who called himself the Mahdi first appeared on the scene, his country had been in the repressive grip of Turko-Egyptian rule since its conquest by Mehemet Ali, Viceroy of Egypt, some sixty years earlier in 1820-22. Graft and extortion were common, the countryside was ravaged by slave traders, and the populace was controlled with the whip and the sword.

Mohammed Ahmed ibn-Sayyid Abdullah's history is obscure until 1881, when at the age of thirty-seven — on Abba Island, a hundred and fifty miles upstream from Khartoum — he declared himself the deliverer who the prophet Mohammed had promised would some day appear. A member of a Moslem order of warrior-priests, he attracted followers first by the score, then by the hundred, and soon by the thousand. Accepted as the Mahdi, he declared a *jehad* (holy war) against the corrupt Egyptians. His adherents, the Ansar (later nicknamed "dervishes" by British soldiers, in slang that had originated in the Middle East), were remarkable not only for their numbers but also for their fanaticism. They willingly sought death in battle, having been promised Paradise.

The Mahdi conducted his first campaign in Kordofan, a province of the central Sudan immediately to the southwest of Omdurman and Khartoum. By January 1883 he had captured its capital, El Obeid, a city at the center of ancient trade routes connecting Kordofan and Darfur, the Sudan's westernmost province, with Egypt and the Red Sea. Only a few months previously, however, the

British had invaded and occupied Egypt. While they were not themselves then willing to mount an expedition against the Mahdists, they permitted the Egyptian government they controlled to do so. An Egyptian-recruited force of seven thousand infantrymen, a thousand cavalrymen, and a train of five thousand camels set forth up the Nile to Khartoum under the command of an Englishman in Egypt's employ, Col. William Hicks. Soon after reaching Khartoum, Hicks's ill-prepared army moved into the western desert toward El Obeid. The Mahdi's dervishes fell on it fifty thousand strong in the thorn scrub there and immolated it. No more than two or three hundred Egyptians survived. Save for Khartoum and the river itself, the Sudan belonged to the Mahdi. He now laid siege to Khartoum.

Meanwhile, despite British Prime Minister William Gladstone's disinclination to fight further in Africa, there were those in London who had no wish to see the Sudan lost to Egypt and thus to Great Britain. They maneuvered the government into sending a national military hero on a diplomatic mission to Egypt and Khartoum to save the day. That man was Chinese Gordon, who as Governor General of the Sudan under the Khedive had helped suppress the slave trade in Equatoria, the Sudan's southernmost province. Gordon was a man of curious paradoxes. Devious in his diplomacy yet frank about the broad policies he wished to pursue, indecisive and contradictory in many of his actions yet personally courageous, he was fanatical in the pursuit of what he saw as his duty — a mystic who was also a military man of tremendous physical endurance. Gordon's official instructions were merely to evacuate the foreign population of Khartoum and withdraw the Egyptian garrison there. It is possible that some of those involved in the decision to send Gordon — the more imperialistically-minded members of the British Cabinet — hoped that once he reached Khartoum he would stay there and that, as a result, the British would be forced to intervene militarily to save the day.

If this hope existed, only half of it came true. Once at Khartoum, Gordon evacuated about twenty-five hundred women, children, and wounded. He then *did* proceed to stay in the city, holding out there for almost a year, constantly pleading for relief from the north. Debates raged in the British Cabinet, Parliament, and press, but the help Gordon asked for was never forthcoming. Finally, early on the morning of January 26, 1885, a mass of the Mahdi's dervishes broke through Gordon's undermanned defenses and began a massacre of the city's populace. Gordon — the only Englishman left in Khartoum — met the invaders on the steps of his palace. There they speared him and cut off his head, carrying it away in a white cloth as a trophy for the Mahdi.

The Sudan was abandoned to the rule of the dervishes, although their leader did not long survive his enemy, Gordon. The Mahdi died five months later and was succeeded by his chief aide, the Khalifa (adviser) Abdullah. Under the Khalifa's barbaric rule the Sudan lapsed into a tyranny as savage and corrupt as any ever imposed by foreigners. It has been estimated that during his reign seventy-five per cent of the population was lost through internecine wars, execution at the Khalifa's whim, the slave trade, famine, and epidemics.

The British — including Queen Victoria — regarded Gordon's death as martyrdom, and Mahdism came to be regarded throughout Europe as evil incarnate — a threat to Christianity itself. But it was eleven years before the British acted to move against the Mahdists, and thirteen before a British army actually joined battle with the dervishes. The commander of the army that did so was Gen. Kitchener, and one of his junior officers was a young cavalryman named Winston Churchill. On September 1, 1898, Kitchener's force of twenty thousand men formed for battle on the plain outside Omdurman. At dawn the next morning the Khalifa's entire army of fifty thousand attacked with reckless bravery in a series of savage charges and was quickly and decisively defeated. Within an hour or two the well-prepared British had killed some ten thousand Mahdist soldiers at a cost to themselves of only four hundred casualties. The Khalifa retired from the field with the remnants of his troops. He was caught a year later near Abba Island, where the Mahdi had first preached his gospel. Surrounded by his emirs, the Khalifa was cut down by a force under Maj. F. R. Wingate and buried where he died. To Wingate's report Kitchener added: "Mahdism is now a thing of the past, and I hope that a brighter era has now opened for the Sudan."

Kitchener almost immediately set about the task of seeing that his hope became reality. As a start, he rebuilt Khartoum, laying it out in the form of the Union Jack, less out of chauvinism than because the result of the straight intersecting avenues could easily be commanded by machine guns. He planted thousands of trees, ordered a bronze statue of Gordon to be set up in the center of the city (where it remained for half a century), and had a palace befitting his position constructed for himself. Kitchener's gunboat, the *Melik,* still rides at anchor in the river by the city, although it has now been retired to peaceful service as headquarters for the Blue Nile Sailing Club.

At Khartoum the Blue Nile (Bahr el Azraq) meets the White Nile at the river's most important junction. The shape of this confluence gives the city its name; *khartoum* is Arabic for elephant's trunk. From this point on to the Mediterranean the river is known for nineteen hundred miles as the Nile. The only further accession of water it receives is from the Atbara River, which joins it a few hundred miles to the north, for there is virtually no rainfall between Khartoum and the sea.

The waters of the Blue Nile are darker-hued than those of the White Nile, but they are not blue. Where the two rivers meet the difference in coloration is immediately apparent: The former is a greenish brown, the latter a dirty gray. When the Blue Nile is not in flood the waters of the streams slide along side by side until eventually they mingle just beyond Khartoum. For six months of the year the Blue Nile is in flood, and then it overwhelms the White Nile with its greater volume and swifter current. It contributes sixty-three per cent of the Nile's total flow, and it bears a fine silt upon which the riverine agriculturalists long were supposed to have depended to renew their soil. An American survey team testing the Blue Nile's silt near the river's source in Ethiopia, however, has been unable to make anything grow in it. Thus it may be possible that the mud of the White Nile is, after all, the real mainspring of life in the Nile valley.

No one has ever been able, either on water or by land, to follow the full course of the Blue Nile from its source in the Ethiopian province of Bagemder down to the desert. Falls and rapids make passage by boat impossible; gorges as deep as a mile — where the river cuts through the central massif — make even walking along the Blue Nile inconceivable. The river leaves the southern end of Lake Tana (which is 1400 square miles in area) and drops 4500 feet before it enters the Sudan, 470 miles away. The Blue Nile's floods are caused by the high rainfall at its watershed — sixty inches a year, compared with forty-seven inches for the White Nile — and provide the major portion of the water needed for the irrigation system so important to both Egypt and the Sudan.

The first part of that system of water control rises just above Sennar, on the Blue Nile approximately two hundred miles southeast of Khartoum. Here a wall of stone two miles long restrains the river's flow. The dam was designed in 1913 with the enthusiastic backing of Kitchener (then back in England), begun in 1919, and finished six years later at a cost of close to $20,000,000. Its purpose is to irrigate the Gezira, a triangle of land between the Blue and White Niles. Although the million or so acres of the Gezira project receive only a meager eight to twenty inches of rain a year, they bear the Sudan's major money crop: a long-staple cotton. From the Sennar Dam water is fed to a network of canals totaling 9400 miles in length. Along them more than 26,000 families raise the cotton and share in the profits as partners with the government. The area also produces wheat and other food crops, but it is on the sale of cotton from the Gezira, more than on any other one factor, that the economy of the nation depends. The Sudan exports other commodities — peanuts, sesame seed, dates, and eighty-five per cent of the world's gum arabic, as well as exotica like ivory, ostrich feathers, and leopard skins — and sells some camels, sheep, and goats to Egypt for meat. But the proceeds realized from the sale of all these items would not support the country. It is high prices in the world's cotton markets that bring prosperity to the Sudan.

The Republic of the Sudan is encouraging a diversity of industries, however. It has built three aluminum plants in recent years, manufactures 150,000,000 cigarettes annually, and is trying to utilize the great quantities of papyrus in the Sudd for paper-making. Internal trade is brisk, as a visit to the *suk* (market) of any Sudanese town makes clear. Given the stolidity and stamina of its sturdy people, and its determination to develop its resources, the Sudan is likely to flourish as long as there is water in the Nile.

Plates

87

A young girl of the Hamar tribe, from the Kordofan region north of the Sudd, which had migrated to the Nile near Malakal, where this picture was taken. She is wearing a leather amulet containing sacred writings from the Koran transcribed by a holy man.   [1947]

88-89

A swarm of locusts above the marshes of the White Nile near El Jebelein, north of Malakal. These insects, which can devour every green thing in their path, have swarmed over the Nile for centuries. ("For they covered the whole earth, so that the land was darkened; and they did eat every herb of the land.") Even with modern insecticides the Sudanese have been unable to get rid of them completely.   [1947]

90

Top: The sandy shore of the White Nile at El Jebelein. The villagers wear the typical cotton garment and white turban of the Sudanese Arabs. *Bottom:* Thorny acacia trees on the banks of the White Nile at El Jebelein cast a welcome shade. The little boy at the far left is carrying river water in two old gasoline tins. Tied on the donkey in the foreground are two large mudfish, perhaps caught from the felucca moored close by.   [Both 1947]

91

A large borassus palm tree in the center of the market place at El Jebelein. Cotton, grains (chiefly durra, a sorghum millet), and gum arabic are sold here, as well as sheep, goats, and camels — both live and as meat.   [1947]

92

Two women winnowing grain in the Gezira district, between the White and Blue Niles. The kernels settle in the trays while the chaff flies off. The Gezira Scheme, begun in 1925, was one of the most far-sighted agricultural projects undertaken in colonial Africa and is today the backbone of the Sudanese economy.   [1947]

93

Top: Sudanese bathing in the waters of the Blue Nile near the Sennar Dam, 150 miles southeast of Khartoum. The animal skins in the foreground

have been filled with water and will be transported to the villages on donkeys. *Bottom:* A Nilometer on the Blue Nile at Wad Medani, ninety miles from Khartoum. Sudanese gauge the height of the Nile by the steps of the Nilometer and from this predict the height of the annual floods. The ancient Egyptians also built Nilometers, usually by cutting lines on a smooth rock on the river's edge.   [Both 1947]

94

The late Sir Sayed Abdel Rahman el Mahdi Pasha, son of the Mahdi who led the dervishes in the 1880's, photographed before the cupola in Omdurman which was once part of his father's tomb. It is topped by the Islamic crescent cut through by a broad stabbing spear, the emblem of the original Mahdi.   [1947]

94-95

The market at Omdurman, showing stalls with galvanized iron roofs supported by wooden frames. As at markets throughout most of the Sudan, it is possible to buy a great variety of camels here, at prices sometimes as low as ten dollars.   [1959]

96

An aerial view of the confluence of the Blue and White Niles, looking westward. The Blue Nile, in the foreground, sweeps in a wide arc to meet the White Nile which flows (from left to right) under the railroad bridge in the middle distance. On the far left is Khartoum, the capital city; on the far right is Khartoum North, an industrial suburb; and on the other side of the bridge is Omdurman.   [1947]

97

The light smooth surface of the White Nile as it is joined at Khartoum by the darker waters of the Blue Nile on the right. The fishermen on the banks stand in crude rowboats and cast their round nets into the shallow waters.   [1947]

98

A felucca, the single-masted sailboat prevalent on the Nile. Traveling south, the sails are usually furled while the current carries the boat; traveling north, a prevailing north wind moves it against the current.   [1947]

94

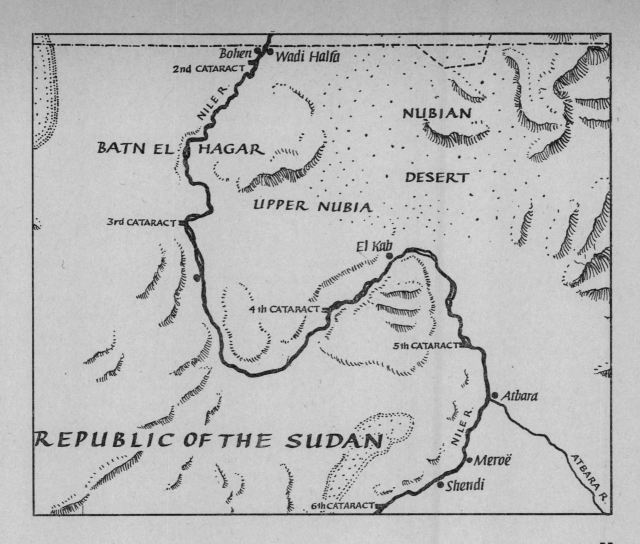

V
Upper Nubia

Six so-called cataracts — actually a series of rapids caused by dark, polished transverse ribs of rock jutting up from the desert floor — disturb the serenity of the Nile's northward flow from Khartoum through Upper and Lower Nubia to Aswan in southern Egypt. The only navigable stretch of this section of the Nile extends from the First Cataract at Aswan to the Second at Wadi Halfa near the Egyptian-Sudanese border. (The Cataracts are numbered from Aswan southward, since this was the direction in which the explorers who first encountered them were traveling.) The five southernmost Cataracts lie in the Sudan, the first of them to occur in the Nile's course to the sea (the Sixth) at the Sabaloka Gorge, less than a hundred miles north of Khartoum. Only two of the Cataracts — the First and Second — are at all impressive physically. As natural phenomena, they are overshadowed by the vast, barren landscape that extends into the horizon from both their eastern and western banks.

To drive out of Khartoum in any direction is to encounter desert within a very few miles. This is not the soft sand-dune desert of the Sahara that one sees nearer the Nile farther north, but a hard, dusty terrain, dotted with thorny acacia bushes and small rocks, shimmering in the distance with the pulsation of a mirage. In the hot season the desert here is swept by the *haboob,* a dust storm that rises without warning. Fine gritty dust attacks the mouth, eyes, and nostrils of the unfortunate traveler and seems to join earth and heaven in one dark, ominous wall.

In the primeval sands of the Nubian Desert and the sterile reaches of land south of it are hidden the relics of millennia of history. The Pharaohs once ruled Nubia, the Land of Gold, as far south as the Fourth Cataract and extracted revenues from it in the form of gold and slaves. Fragments of copper and pottery belonging to Egypt's Fourth Dynasty (2900-2750 B.C.) have recently been unearthed in a "lost city" on the site of the present Sudanese village of Bohen, near the Second

Cataract, indicating that the Egyptians must have been settled there during that time. Some sixteen centuries or so later their dominion had become so weakened that the Libians, marching southeast along a chain of oases, were able to occupy the land of Cush, in the Nile valley area of the present Egyptian-Sudanese border, and colonize it. The vigor of the Cushites was such that in 712 B.C. they were strong enough to invade Egypt itself, where the power of the Pharaohs had been in decline for over a thousand years.

The Cushites — or Nubians — established themselves as rulers of the Nile from Khartoum to the Delta in a comparatively short-lived regime (712-663 B.C.) known as the Ethiopian Dynasty. They in turn were overcome by the invading Assyrians and withdrew to their capital of Meroë, where the more than two hundred low pyramids they built still rise from the desert floor. Protected by the Nile, the city long proved impregnable to invaders. From their fortress there, the Meroitic kings and queens held sway over the greater part of the northern Sudan for another six hundred years. In the first century A.D., Meroites again invaded Egypt. This time they encountered more formidable opposition, however, for Egypt was now under Roman rule, and the Romans had every intention of extending their empire to the south. The Romans beat back the Meroites. But even the power of Rome could not conquer the Nile. Its armies were stopped by the Cataracts, and in 300 A.D. the Emperor Diocletian finally decided to abandon Nubia. Despite this withdrawal, the Kingdom of Meroë was doomed to disappear. In the middle of the fourth century A.D. a migration of other Nubian tribes eastward out of the wastes of Kordofan ended its sway.

In the sixth century A.D. the Nubians turned to Christianity, encouraged by the Byzantine Emperor Justinian I, who hoped that conversion would curb their spirit. So strongly did they hold to their new faith that when the Islamic invasion of 630 A.D. swept over Syria and Egypt and into the Sudan, the Nubians concluded a treaty with the Moslems that left Nubia Christian for six hundred years.

Toward the end of the fifteenth century a new power appeared out of the east — a horde of black warriors who called themselves the Fung. They are thought to have come from Ethiopia, although their name corresponds to no ethnic group there. In 1504 they made their capital at Sennar on the Blue Nile and began to extend the borders of their empire to the northeast into Kordofan. By the end of the seventeenth century they had become devoutly Moslem. Their kings ruled in great state, wearing robes heavy with gold and surrounding themselves with slaves. The Fung Empire carried on trade with places as far away as India. Protected by a force of cavalrymen who wore shirts of steel chain mail and helmets of burnished copper, the Fung proved invincible for hundreds of years. None the less, of all their civilization practically nothing remains, for they built of mud.

The Fung were destroyed by an implacable adversary: Mehemet Ali, the ruthless, efficient ruler of Egypt from 1805 to 1848. At the time of the Fungs' decline Egypt was nominally a province of the Ottoman Empire; Mehemet Ali professed token fealty to the Turks but gradually strengthened his position to the point where he wielded independent power. Jealous of the wealth of the Fung empire, he dispatched a force of four thousand Turks and Armenians, under the command of his third son, Ismail, to appropriate the gold mines of Fazoghli, south of Sennar, and enslave the population. In June 1821, Badi, the last of the Fung kings, surrendered to Ismail, and a dynasty came to an end. After a futile campaign against other groups in the Sudan that lasted two years, Ismail turned back toward Egypt. In October 1822 he reached Shendi, a Nile town a hundred miles down river from Khartoum that had been a dependency of the Fung, and there was burned to death by the inhabitants. In reprisal, Mehemet Ali ravaged the northern Sudan from end to end; in one year his men brutally killed fifty thousand Sudanese and razed every sizable town they encountered.

The market at Shendi was once one of the busiest in Africa, bestriding as it did two of the chief trade routes through the Sudan. It is still a bustling place where local produce like dates, grain, and crude rope are displayed next to the more sophisticated commodities produced by modern industry. Beyond it lie the tombs and other ruins of Meroë, baked by the desert heat. The temperature here rises as high as 120 degrees Fahrenheit and for several months in summer does not drop below 104.

It is a dry heat, for the area's annual rainfall never measures more than an inch, and sometimes not a single drop of rain falls from one year to the next. As a result, life along this part of the Nile is dependent on water from wells, which are scarce, and from the river. Here the Nile begins to describe a great "S" which carries it from Shendi past three of the Cataracts to the hundred-mile stretch called Batn el Hagar (Belly of Rocks) that ends at the Second Cataract outside Wadi Halfa.

The Berbers — as the Nilotes who inhabit this area are now generally called — have apparently changed little in appearance over a period of two thousand years. Though they are now free of the oppressions from which they suffered for so long, survival is still hard for them, at best. Theirs is a male-dominated society, in which the symbols of the bridegroom are the sword, the knife, and the whip (which is made of hippopotamus hide). The Berbers, who still speak their own Nubian language, are a sedentary people who cultivate narrow strips of land along the Nile's banks. The more primitive of their farms are irrigated by means of the *shaduf,* a device introduced into Egypt from Mesopotamia during the Eighteenth Dynasty (1580-1350 B.C.). This ancient machine is nothing more than a long pole with a container suspended from one end, and a counterweight tied to the other. The container is dipped into the river, the pole is raised and pivoted, and the water is poured into an irrigation ditch. Using a shaduf, one man in one day can provide water for a quarter of an acre. More complicated, and less common, is the *saqia* a form of waterwheel driven by an ox, or sometimes by a donkey or a camel.

Here and there along this section of the Nile more advanced systems of irrigation have been developed. When the river is in full flood, the overflow is fed through canals into basins enclosed by low walls. A series of ditches between the basins distributes the water and ensures an even deposit of the rich silt it carries. When the flood subsides, crops are planted and harvested. Then the fields lie fallow for half a year. Dried out by the sun, they soon crack, which permits the all-important aeration of the soil.

Even these agricultural efforts produce only a modest amount of grains, beans, and lentils, however, and many Berberine men are forced to look for work elsewhere in the Sudan and Egypt. They often find it in governmental or commercial offices, in jobs as boatmen or drivers, or in domestic service. Working away from home, they learn Arabic. (That language, in fact, is now being taught in the schools in Nubia and thus is gradually replacing the ancient tongue.)

Over the centuries, much has changed in Nubia. Soon even the landscape will be altered by the hand of man; for when the new High Dam is finished at Aswan it will back up the Nile's waters as far south as the Third Cataract, two hundred miles upstream from the Egyptian-Sudanese border. The town of Wadi Halfa, long the gateway to the Sudan, will disappear beneath the dammed-up Nile into history.

Plates

103

A young Arab girl from the Kordofan region — with typical tribal scars and kohl-rimmed eyes — drawing water from a well just north of Khartoum, near the Sixth Cataract. Since women in this area are extremely shy of strangers, this close-up was made with a telephoto lens. [1959]

104-105

Top: A herder driving his flock of sheep southward toward Omdurman, where they will be slaughtered for the market. The stretch of land here, unnurtured by the Nile, is extremely desolate and barren, with only a few acacia trees for shade. *Bottom:* A model farm north of Khartoum, supplied with water from the Nile by two modern pumps working twelve hours a day to irrigate the 350 acres under cultivation. The oxen in the foreground are threshing wheat with modern iron rollers which cut the stalks into small pieces. [Both 1947]

106-107

Part of the market at Shendi, on the Nile some hundred miles north of Khartoum. Once at the crossroads of two great trade routes and a center for the slave trade, the city now has only a small market, where grain, dates, rope, wood, and other products are sold. [1947]

108

The low pyramids of Meroë in the desert on the east bank of the Nile, about 200 air miles (and more than 450 river miles) north of Khartoum. Insignificant in size compared with Egypt's pyramids, they none the less mark the site of a major ancient civilization. [1947]

109

Bas-reliefs on a ruined chapel in the North Cemetery of Meroë. Thirty-four kings, two crowned princes, and five queens were buried here, though all forty-one pyramids, like the ones in this photograph, are now in general disrepair. [1947]

110

A wide stretch of the Nile amid the rocks of the Second Cataract, some of which can be seen jutting from the river in the background. The man standing in the boat, quieting his donkey as his sons row him across the water, is a Nubian. [1947]

111

A *shaduf* on the banks of the Nile, with one of the ubiquitous gasoline cans being used to lift the water. The vegetables at the edge of the water were planted after the fall floods receded and have received their quota of water. [1947]

112-113

The Batn el Hagar (Belly of Rocks) at the Second Cataract; the course of the Nile is interfered with for six rocky miles. As is evident from the twisting paths of the water in the middle distance, this cataract is not navigable. [1947]

113

The Nile waters as they enter the Second Cataract, seen from Abu Sir, a hill overlooking the region. Along this part of the Nile the desert itself often forms the banks of the river, as in the foreground of this photograph. [1947]

114

A painted house front in the town of Halfa Digheim, a village near the Second Cataract that will be covered by water from Egypt's High Dam. This type of decoration, found on many houses in the Sudan, is painted on dried clay applied to the original surface in low relief. [1947]

115

A young Berber girl at Kokki, a village near the Second Cataract. She is wearing the black cotton costume customary among the women of Upper Nubia and is adorned with a silver necklace and leather amulets around her neck; the silver ring in her nose is called a *nibla*. [1947]

116-117

Young boys, in attitudes ranging from mock-fighting to a British-style salute, pose before a house in Wadi Halfa, on the Sudan-Egypt border. The drawings and inscriptions on the wall behind them indicate that the owner of the house has made the sacred pilgrimage to Mecca. [1947]

118

Mohammed Seliman, a Nubian who has traveled far from his native village in the Sudan to find employment, seen here at Idfu, north of Aswan, in Egypt. The white turban, called an *imma,* is worn by all Sudanese men. [1947]

104

117

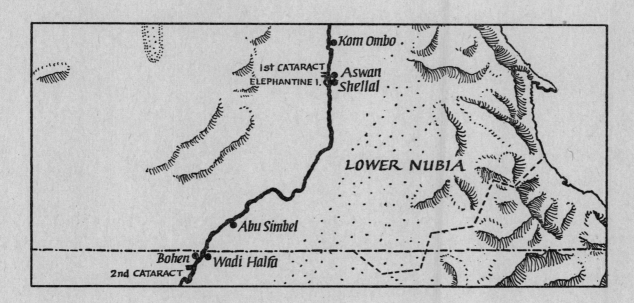

VI
The Rising
Waters

Between the First Cataract at Aswan and the Second Cataract at Wadi Halfa the world of the Pharaohs and the age of modern technology meet. Nowhere else along the whole length of the Nile do past and future so strive against each other to capture men's minds and energies. The completion of the High Dam will mean the loss of whatever antiquities cannot be salvaged beforehand; it will also make impossible the investigation of many sites that have not yet been studied by archaeologists. On the other hand, it will turn nearly two million acres of desert in Egypt into arable land, and permit a larger measure of industrialization through the generating of electricity. The Sudan, too, will benefit.

Just past the Sudan border in Egypt the Nile meets the first group of major relics threatened by the forthcoming rising of its waters — in particular, two temples dug into a long hill of sandstone at Abu Simbel thirty-two centuries ago by Ramses II (1292-1225 B.C.). Each is set in an angle of the cliffs on the river's west bank, the larger temple upstream from the smaller one.

The larger temple penetrates one hundred and eighty feet into the rock. Four seated colossi of Ramses, each more than sixty-five feet high, are carved from the cliff face and dominate the temple's façade. Within, the first large room is a hypostyle hall in which rise eight columns, each thirty feet high and depicting an aspect of the god Osiris; one of them represents Ramses II assuming the appearance of Osiris and wearing the double crown of Upper and Lower Egypt. Bas-reliefs tell the story of the Pharaoh's victories over the Assyrians. Among modern travelers, the first to describe the temple was the Swiss-born explorer Johann Ludwig Burckhardt, who in 1813 clambered up the drifts of sand that almost obscured the colossi to measure an ear on one of them. From its size he deduced what eventually proved to be the correct height of the gigantic statues, though at that time only their heads were visible.

Burckhardt was able to be more explicit about the smaller temple at Abu Simbel, for there the colossi (six of them in a façade ninety feet long and forty feet high) stared from the graven rock in full exposure, as they do today. Four are figures of Ramses II; the other two, of his favorite wife, Nefertari. Around the king's feet, in deep bas-relief, are shown some of his children; he had, in fact, a hundred and sixty, the combined progeny of wives and concubines. Between two of the thirty-foot figures, Burckhardt found an entrance, but it was cluttered with debris. Local tribesmen were using the temple as a refuge, and Burckhardt did not want to disturb them, so he missed the painted bas-reliefs inside. Like the other treasures at Abu Simbel, the bas-reliefs are now threatened with inundation.

Italian engineers have developed an ingenious plan to save the temples. Their proposal is to cut both from the mountain in two great blocks of sandstone, encasing each block in reinforced concrete and then raising it two hundred feet, stage by stage, by means of three hundred hydraulically controlled jacks, with pillars inserted at intervals. The project would take six years to complete and would cost $45,000,000. Unfortunately, it seems unlikely that the money required to put the plan into effect can be raised.

The Nile's waters will start to back up as far south as Abu Simbel in 1964. The site of the dam itself is at Sadd el Aali, some two hundred miles downstream from Abu Simbel and upstream from the original dam at Aswan. The old dam was built by the British in 1902 and has twice since been heightened. Between the old dam and the site of the new one lies the second major area of archaeological interest that will mostly be inundated: a group of twelve islands scattered across a broad reach of the river at the head of the First Cataract. The largest of these is Bigeh, but the most important to antiquarians is Philae, Pearl of the Nile — a low island that covers seventeen acres rich with green growth during the summer months. Philae was a center for the worship of Osiris — the god who symbolized fertility and rebirth and thus the Nile itself — and of his wife, Isis.

Philae is covered for part of the year by the waters stored behind the old Aswan Dam and emerges into view only when the sluices of the dam are open from July to October. The oldest buildings on the island were raised by Nectanebo I and his successor Nectanebo II, both Pharaohs of the fourth century B.C. These structures are less imposing, though, than the temple of Isis, built by the Ptolemy Pharaohs two centuries later, which immersion has not noticeably injured. In addition to these buildings, there remain the ruins of some temples built by the Greek and Roman conquerors of Egypt. The temple of Isis and the other monuments on Philae are to be permanently protected by cofferdams designed by the Dutch; the United States has pledged $6,000,000 toward the project. One effect of the High Dam will be to stabilize the Nile's flow down to the old dam, so that the cofferdams' low retaining walls will preserve Philae when the High Dam is completed in 1968.

Downstream from Philae, where the river flashes and swirls over the granite rocks of the First Cataract, the character of the landscape changes. The Nile emerges from the confinement of harsh escarpments and barren sands into a pastoral countryside where the earth is more fertile. Shrubs and palms rise above rice paddies and fields of wheat. The forces of nature here seem far less harsh.

Beyond lies Aswan, once one of the southernmost outposts of the Roman Empire. To its market the ancient Egyptians and their overlords sent honey, unguents, beads, and cloth in exchange for the riches of the Sudan: ivory, skins, gold and other minerals, exotic feathers, and domestic animals. Today the seminomadic Bisharin — the lean warriors whom Kipling called "Fuzzy Wuzzies" — still flock into Aswan from the Arabian Desert and the Red Sea Hills, aloof strangers who bring with them wares in the form of livestock and henna leaves.

Plans for the High Dam have already changed forever the lives of thousands of Nubians in the Sudan and Egypt. Wadi Halfa, the Sudanese town at the southern extreme of the new reservoir, will be flooded. As a result, its population is being moved hundreds of miles to the south, down across the desert to the banks of the Atbara River. There, forty-two thousand Sudanese Nubians will be resettled — not without protest — at Khashm el Girba, a new irrigation project. Behind them, under two hundred feet of water, they will leave half a million date palms, their homes, and possibly their very way of life. To the north, the Egyptian Government will relocate sixty thousand Nubians in the Kom Ombo valley to man a new agricultural and industrial complex that is intended to make sugar an important Egyptian export. Forty miles north of Aswan, and the site of the country's largest sugar refinery, the project is already the heart of Egypt's sugar industry.

Power for expanding industry is a major objective of the High Dam. Its twelve turbogenerators will provide 2,000,000 more kilowatts an hour for the increasingly industrialized nations. A new hydro-electric plant, built by Swedish and Swiss engineers, is already producing 345,000 kilowatts an hour. It powers a factory recently built by technicians from West Germany that turns out 1600 tons of fertilizer a day to enrich the acres that have been newly irrigated. In ten years the population of the Aswan has swollen from 28,000 to 48,000; every day more and more labor, skilled and un-skilled, is drawn to the town. The once-quiet Cataract Hotel, which during the Edwardian era was a retreat for wealthy — and usually ageing — expatriates seeking an escape from harsh European winters, now bustles with a comparatively young professional clientele composed of salesmen, archaeologists, and technicians, among others. A sign at the entrance to the lounge reads: "Drinking is compulsory."

Because the construction of the High Dam is being financed by a loan from the Soviet Union, some of the customers at the Cataract Hotel have recently been Russian. The loan amounted to some $300,000,000, repayable at two and a half per cent interest over a twelve-year period, beginning a year after the completing of the dam. The loan contract provides for a dam about 365 feet high, forming a reservoir with a capacity of 32,000,000,000 cubic meters, a power station situated on the diversionary channel, and 1740 miles of high- and low-voltage transmission lines to northern Egypt and the Delta region.

The supply of water from the new High Dam reservoir will be divided between the Republic of the Sudan and the United Arab Republic (as Egypt is now officially known) under the terms of an agreement in November 1959. In 1958 the British and Egyptians apportioned the Nile's waters, with 4,000,000,000 cubic meters going to the Sudan and 48,000,000,000 to Egypt. The Sudan will now get an additional 14,500,000,000 cubic meters; Egypt, an extra 7,500,000,000. Since it is expected that 10,000,000,000 of the 32,000,000,000 cubic meters of water in the reservoir will evaporate, the allotment of the Nile's waters will now be 18,500,000,000 cubic meters for the Sudan, and 55,500,000,000 for Egypt. In addition, the present agreement provides that Egypt will pay the Sudanese population of Wadi Halfa almost $29,000,000 in compensation for their forced move south, and officially recognizes the right of the Sudan to build two new dams (one at Khashm el Girba on the Atbara and the other at Roseires on the Blue Nile). Under joint study for the future are projects at Lake Tana, source of the Blue Nile; at the White Nile's three great lakes, Victoria, Kyoga, and Albert; and at Jonglei, where a canal may some day be constructed to bypass the Sudd.

The future will see the Nile more and more under the constraint of modern engineering methods as it flows to the sea. But paradoxically the direction of its flow in terms of human history is toward the past. Leaving the High Dam and the twentieth century, the river glides between banks littered with relics of that distant age when to the Egyptians the Pharaohs were children of the sun, and their realm — in reality meager and restricted — encompassed the known world. Near Aswan rough obelisks and statues still lie in a granite quarry where slave laborers left them, diverted by some ancient calamity, millennia ago. It took two thousand slaves three years, according to Hero-dotus, to move a single monolith from the Aswan quarries to the Delta. It is impossible to calculate how many more men spent their lives building the temples on Elephantine Island, just below the First Cataract, or cutting into rock to fashion luxurious tombs along the Nile for the rulers who controlled the gateway into Nubia. Only the stone, some of the paint, and a few of the jewels remain. None the less, as the Nile begins to thread its way through Egypt toward the Mediterranean a sense of ancient splendor increasingly pervades its atmosphere.

Plates

123

Façade of the larger temple at Abu Simbel, showing remains of the four seated colossi of Ramses II.   [1947]

124-125

The hypostyle hall at Abu Simbel. Hollow relief (*left*) depicts Ramses II smiting his Asiatic enemies. Column (*right*) shows Ramses II as the god Osiris.   [Both 1947]

126-127

The smaller temple at Abu Simbel. *Left:* The façade with its six colossi. *Right:* Relief showing the children of Ramses II at his feet. The initials "R.C." are the work of some early tourist.   [Both 1947]

128-129

The partly inundated temple of Isis at Philae.   [1947]

130-131

Villagers on Bigeh Island listening to Radio Cairo. The island will be submerged when the new Aswan dam is built.   [1961]

132

Top: An aerial view of the old Aswan dam, looking upstream. *Bottom:* The First Cataract, facing west from the top of the old dam.   [Both 1947]

133

Dynamite blasting a new channel through which the Nile can flow while the High Dam is being built across the main channel.   [1961]

134

The old quarter of Aswan. *Top:* Tattered blankets and burlap bags keep the sun from the store fronts. *Bottom:* Drawing on a wall. [Both 1947]

135

Top: A Bisharin at a nomad camp near Aswan sorting grain for his two camels, who eat from his lap. *Bottom:* A donkey, one of the most valuable animals in Egypt, before a decorated wall in Aswan.   [Both 1947]

136-137

Elephantine Island, seen from the old quarter of Aswan. The columns in the center mark the re-

mains of a temple; at the far left is the recently built tomb of the Aga Khan.   [1961]

138

Tombs near Elephantine Island. *Top:* Exterior of the tomb of Pepi-nakht, a nobleman, cut into the cliffs on the west bank of the Nile. *Bottom:* Two dogs, one of them a greyhound common in ancient Egypt, carved in hollow relief on the tomb of Sirenput I.   [Both 1961]

139

The crude interior of the tomb of Hunu, carved out of the cliffs on the Nile bank near Elephantine Island.   [1961]

140

Unfinished obelisk in the granite quarry of Aswan, from which the ancient Pharaohs took much of their stone. Though much taller than any obelisk in the world now standing, it was never raised because it developed flaws like the long crack still visible on its surface.   [1961]

141

An unfinished colossus from the Aswan quarry, lying just across the river from Shellal, a settlement near the old dam.   [1961]

142

Granite outcroppings of the First Cataract in the Nile near Elephantine Island.   [1961]

142-143

Top: The old Coptic monastery of St. Simeon, near Aswan, abandoned in the thirteenth century.

Bottom: The monastery's ruined interior, showing an excellent vaulted corridor on the right. Little is left of the religious paintings that once adorned the walls and domes.   [Both 1961]

144-145

The town of Rabaswan near Elephantine Island, typical of the many small settlements clustered close to the Nile for hundreds of miles below the First Cataract.   [1961]

146

The Nilometer at Elephantine Island, showing ancient stone steps and modern slotted marble slabs on the walls.   [1961]

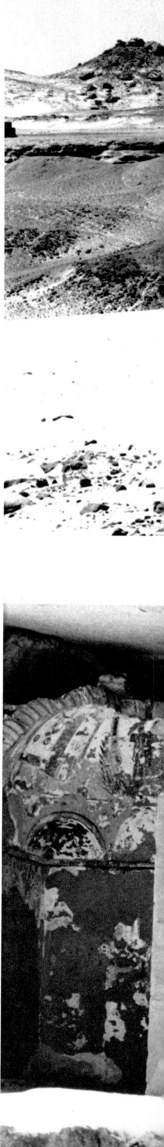

VII
The Green
Thread

The modern traveler in a jet plane streaking north toward Cairo through the cloudless skies of Egypt sees the Nile below Aswan as a green thread. From the spreading mass of vegetation around Kom Ombo, the river runs north through an area of vast brownness. Even the metallic glint of the water and the misty verdure of the cultivation along its banks seem insubstantial and insignificant amid the drab and naked miles of desert that stretch from horizon to horizon. To the east the Arabian Desert, inhabited only by wandering Bisharin with their camels and a few sheep and goats, pushes almost to the river's edge. Westward, the arable land sometimes extends away from the Nile for as much as twelve miles, but beyond lies the Libyan Desert, where nothing thrives but the *jerboa,* or desert rat. In this part of the world only the Nile sustains existence. Today, as it was yesterday and thousands of yesterdays ago, in the words of the Koran, Allah creates all life from water.

There is no rain in this region; thus, all cultivation is the result of irrigation. As early as 3400 B.C. the ancient Egyptians tried to bring life to their sterile acres by means of irrigation canals. However, the first serious attempt at large-scale irrigation was undertaken in 1816 by the ruthless but imaginative Mehemet Ali, who had four hundred thousand male slaves and their families under his command. His purpose was to make cotton an important Egyptian cash crop.

For more than a century thereafter, the ownership of land in Egypt followed a feudal pattern, with most of it in the hands of the pashas (a wealthy class, originally all high military and civil officials). When the pashas' power was broken in 1952 by the revolution engineered by Col. Gamal Abdel Nasser, the latter's promise of agrarian reform attracted widespread support among the *fellahin,* or peasants, who were promised land. Some five hundred thousand acres have now been distributed among a hundred thousand families — a total of half a million people — who were formerly landless. No Egyptian today may own more than one hundred acres of arable land, but even this amount can bring in almost $6,000 a year if properly farmed. The biggest block in the way of agrarian progress is that only four per cent of Egypt's total area of 386,200 square miles is fit for settling or cultivation, and this four per cent — an area the size of Maryland — must support a population of twenty-seven million people.

As it does elsewhere in the world, the population increase in Egypt poses a problem at once urgent and complex. More and more acres are being planted with cotton, an export crop, because of the need for foreign exchange, yet the population soars and thus increases the demand for food-crop acreage. Since 1900 Egypt's population has doubled; by 1970 it is expected to total thirty million, and by the end of the century to rise to more than fifty million. As a result, the new farm land created by the waters from the High Dam will serve only to keep pace with this growth and cannot be expected to cure any basic ills of the Egyptian economy. Nevertheless, the lot of the fellahin has improved. Although the nation's average per capita income is a mere $115 a year, at least prices are fairly stable. Moreover, the government's development schemes include the formation of co-operatives and the building of community centers, clinics, hospitals, and schools. And while the peasant's diet is not an elaborate one, he does not starve.

It was not always so. Although there was no shortage of fertile land five thousand years ago, and Egypt could theoretically import all her grain, the country was seared by famine from time to time; such periods of famine are recorded in the Old Testament. Even in times of comparative prosperity, the lot of the common man was a hard one. Unable or indisposed for one reason or another to revolt, he spent his passion instead in religion. Today the peasant at Kom Ombo who follows the threading movements of the Egyptian stick dance is stamping and striking on ground where in ancient times his ancestors worshiped a score of gods.

Twenty-five miles north of Aswan, the Nile — traveling through the Kom Ombo area now being developed — bends past the temple of Kom Ombo, built by the Ptolemies, those Pharaohs of Greek descent who followed Alexander the Great as rulers of Egypt. When the Romans succeeded the Greeks as masters of Egypt in 30 B.C. they altered the temple. The Emperor Tiberius, for example, added a forecourt (which has since fallen into the Nile). The purity of the classic Egyptian architecture was thus lost, though some elements — the temple's columns in particular, shaped like the papyrus stalks and topped by lotus-blossom capitals — still retain the Egyptian style.

Originally Kom Ombo was the center of the cult of Setekh, a crocodile god who represented Upper Egypt, just as Horus, a sun god, represented Lower Egypt. Toward the end of the Fifth Dynasty, the new cult of Osiris — a sun god identified not only with the forces of fertility but with the underworld and immortality — spread across Egypt. Horus, the hawk-headed, was introduced into Osiris's cycle as his son. Setekh, also entering the pantheon, became the slayer of his father, (or, in another version of the myth, his brother) Osiris, who in turn was avenged by Horus. Osiris thus represented the dead king; Horus, the living king.

Downstream from Kom Ombo, on a little plain at Idfu, stands the temple of Horus, in an almost perfect state of preservation; it is the best-preserved example of Ptolemaic architecture in Egypt. The Nile reaches it through narrows no more than eighty or ninety yards wide. Here the sandstone of Nubia gives place to limestone, though the temple itself is built of the former. Begun in 237 B.C., it was completed a hundred and eighty years later. Two great pylons mark the entrance. Inside, the hypostyle hall opens into another hall of columns, and beyond that is a sanctuary where Horus's hawk eyes once stared out from the darkness and the black sacrificial stone lay cold in the gloom.

The temple celebrates not only the sky god Horus but also his wife, the sky goddess Hathor, the cow-headed patroness of festivities, the dance, and love. Since the center of her cult lay near the necropolis of Thebes, she was later worshiped as "Lady of the West," or queen of the region of the dead. The Nile, entering her domain north of the town of Isna, forms the eastern boundary of that region. There, between the river and the sun-baked hills of the desert, lie — rank on rank — many of the kings of ancient Egypt and members of their courts, commemorated by the greatest collection of temples and tombs known to man: the burial grounds of Thebes.

THE RULERS OF ANCIENT EGYPT *
(All dates B.C.)

OLD KINGDOM (First through Sixth Dynasties)

Accession of Menes	3400-(3500?)
First and Second Dynasties (Thinite)	3400-2980
Third Dynasty (Memphite)	2980-2900
Zoser	
Snefru	
Fourth Dynasty (Memphite)	2900-2750
Khufu (or Cheops)	
Khafre	
Menkure	
Fifth Dynasty (Memphite)	2750-2625
Sixth Dynasty (Memphite)	2625-2475
Pepi I	
Pepi II (reigned ninety years)	
Seventh and Eighth Dynasties (Memphite)	2475-2445

MIDDLE KINGDOM (Ninth through Seventeenth Dynasties)

Ninth and Tenth Dynasties (Heracleopolitan)	2445-2160
Eleventh Dynasty (Theban)	2160-2000
Nibhepetre Mentuhotep IV	
Twelfth Dynasty (Theban)	2000-1788
Amenemhet I	2000-1970
Sesostris (partial co-regency with father)	1980-1935
Amenemhet II (partial co-regency with father)	1938-1903
Sesostris II (partial co-regency with father)	1906-1887
Sesostris III	1887-1849
Amenemhet III	1849-1801
Thirteenth Dynasty (Theban)	
Fourteenth Dynasty (Xoite)	
Fifteenth and Sixteenth Dynasties (Hyksos or "Shepherd Kings")	
Seventeenth Dynasty (Theban)	1788-1580

NEW KINGDOM (Eighteenth through Twentieth Dynasties)

Eighteenth Dynasty (Diospolite)	1580-1350
Ahmose I	1580-1557
Amenhotep I	1557
Thutmose I	
Thutmose II and Queen Hatshepsut	
Thutmose III	1557-1447
Amenhotep II	1447-1420
Thutmose IV	1420-1411
Amenhotep III	1411-1375
Ikhnaton (or Amenhotep IV)	1375-1358
Tutankhamen	c. 1358
Nineteenth Dynasty (Diospolite)	1350-1200
Harmhab	1350-1315
Seti I	1313-1292
Ramses II	1292-1225
Merneptah	1225-1215
Seti II	1209?-1205
Twentieth Dynasty (Diospolite)	1200-1090
Ramessides (Ramses III—XII), especially Ramses III (1198—1167)	1198-1090
Twenty-first Dynasty (Tanite)	1090- 945

NEW KINGDOM

Twenty-second Dynasty (Bubastite)	945-745
Sheshonk I	945-924
Osorkon I	924-895
Osorkon II	874-853
Twenty-third Dynasty (Tanite)	745-718
Twenty-fourth Dynasty (Saite)	718-712
Twenty-fifth Dynasty (Ethiopian)	712-663
Twenty-sixth Dynasty (Saite)	663-525
Psamtik I	663-609
Necho II	609-593
Psamtik II	593-588
Apries	588-569
Twenty-seventh to Thirtieth Dynasties (Persian)	525-332

(During this period Egypt was a Persian province. It was conquered by Alexander the Great in 332.)

PTOLEMIES

Ptolemy I—XIV	323-30
Cleopatra VII (or VI) (partial co-regencies)	51-49, 48-30

* Based on the chronology developed by the late great Egyptologist, James Henry Breasted, as presented in the latest (1958) edition of *Webster's Biographical Dictionary.*

Plates

151
Egyptian farmers performing a stick dance at
Kom Ombo, twenty-five miles north of Aswan,
in the heart of the region that will be developed
by waters from the High Dam. The building in
the background is the railroad station — a modern, and inferior, imitation of the ancient temple
nearby. [1961]

152-153
Carved columns of the temple at Kom Ombo,
built by the Ptolemies in the last centuries before
Christ and later added to by the Roman rulers
of Egypt. Most of the roof of the temple (top)
has collapsed. Bottom right: The carving on this
capital is typical of the Ptolemaic period.
[Both 1961]

154-155
The temple of Horus at Idfu, downstream from
Kom Ombo. The entrance is flanked by pylons
144 feet high; the façade is almost 250 feet wide.
Its monumental size can be seen by comparison
with the white-turbaned guards standing at the
entrance. The carved figures at the extreme left
and right of the pylons are Ptolemy Auletes,
whose forefathers began the temple. Bottom right:
A large granite hawk depicting the sun god Horus, one of the two statues seen above, left, in
front of the temple. [Both 1947]

156-157
The forecourt of the temple at Idfu. The columns
and both the inner and outer walls of the temple
are covered with bas-relief carvings. The faces
on several of the relief figures were chipped
away by early Christians, who attacked many
of the monuments of ancient Egypt. [1947]

157
The two sides of the Narmer palette, found at
Hierakonpolis near Idfu and now in the Cairo
Museum. The plaque commemorates the victories
of Narmer, a Pharaoh of the First Dynasty (c.
3200 B.C.). The front of the palette (top) shows
Narmer marching onto the field of battle to
inspect his beheaded enemies, on the right in the
upper panel. The central panel shows two mythi-
cal animals, whose entwined necks form the well
of the palette. The reverse side (bottom) shows
the Pharaoh smiting a prisoner with his mace.

The horned heads at the very top of each side
of the plaque represent the goddess Hathor, wife
of Horus. [1947]

158-159
The Nile at El Kab, downstream from Aswan.
Along this stretch of the river the desert, visible
in the background, hems in the river on both
sides. The cracked earth in the foreground is a
common sight along the banks after the flood
waters have receded. [1961]

160-161
An Egyptian farmer weeding his cornfield at Isna,
a hundred miles north of Aswan. The field has
been divided into small plots with little mud walls
designed to hold in water and control irrigation.
Behind the farmer is one of the broad canals
leading from the Nile; the two shadufs raise the
water to the fields. [1947]

162
A farmer in the village of Manchat Ammari, near
Luxor, winnowing grain in a manner that dates
back to the time of the Pharaohs. [1947]

163
Top: Ahmed Bey el Ammari, the mayor and
principal landowner of Manchat Ammari. The
man in the photograph on the facing page works
on the mayor's farm. Bottom: Farmers carrying
woven baskets filled with sand to reinforce the
dikes along the Nile at Armant, southwest of
Luxor. In the foreground, their overseer keeps a
watchful eye on them. Dikes control the flow
of the water during flood time. [Both 1947]

164-165
Feluccas at anchor at twilight on the east bank
of the Nile near the site of ancient Thebes. On
this side of the river is the "region of the dead,"
the vast burial ground of the New Kingdom
Pharaohs. [1961]

166
Mummy of Ramses II, now in the Cairo Museum.
The body of this renowned sovereign (probably
the Pharaoh of the Biblical oppression) was mummified by the usual method and has turned black
after being exposed to the air. [1962]

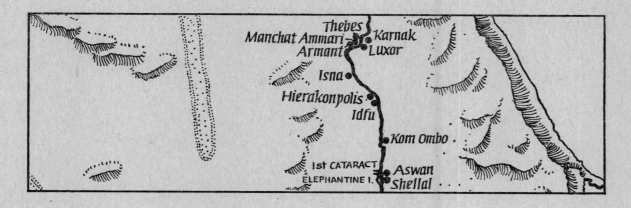

VIII
The Living and
the Land of
the Dead

When Thebes was the capital of the Western world — almost a thousand years before Rome emerged from a state of wilderness in the eighth century B.C. — the river Nile had already been venerated for its fertility over a period of centuries. For centuries, too, it had been an artery vital to the development of commerce and political power. Down river to Thebes from the hot south came oils and jewels, gold, slaves, rare woods, and strange beasts. Up river to Thebes from the Mediterranean islands and the coastline of the Levant came silks, wine, copper, iron, and gold from the mines of Sinai and Tauris. As the vessels bearing these cargoes of tribute, gifts, and merchandise toiled against the current, they often passed flat barges carrying obelisks from the granite quarries of Aswan and great blocks of sandstone to be carved on some Egyptian temple wall near Thebes. Fleets of feluccas sailed north and south along the Nile with grain, vegetables, and carcasses to feed not only the Theban nobility and priesthood, but also their thousands of dependents. All-powerful Thebes sucked in the riches of its surrounding world and gave out little in return.

The social structure of Thebes formed a pyramid, at whose apex glittered the Pharaoh in all his glory. Yet in a sense that pyramid's foundation was mere water. The economy of Thebes, like that of Egypt today, depended on the Nile. In Thebes, the seasons were measured by the Nile's height. When there was drought, it was accompanied by hesitancy and fear on the part of the populace; when the floods came, wild enthusiasm reigned. The arrival of the swelling waters was the signal for bacchanalia. According to Egyptian myth the Nile was then a young lover taking physical possession of his mistress, the dry earth. At such a time, religious observances in Thebes required copious use of the river's spreading brown waters. The remains of two ranks of ram-headed sphinxes line the route from the great temple of Khonsu at Karnak, in the north part of the ancient city, down to the river bank where once the Pharaohs and their priests performed their rites. Even today — although Islam has replaced the old religion — Egyptians often purify themselves with Nile water before their devotions.

Thebes, which earlier had been the capital of Upper Egypt, became the chief city of an Egypt at the height of its prestige and power with the advent of the Eighteenth Dynasty, the beginning of the period known as the New Kingdom. Having crushed the hated Shepherd Kings, the Hyksos, in the Nile Delta, Ahmose I, the dynasty's founder, inaugurated a regime at Thebes that was as successful in peace as in war. Thebes was bisected by the Nile; it no longer exists as an entity, although remnants of its past glory are scattered on and beyond both of the river's banks. On the Nile's east bank remain the magnificent structures of the city's Luxor and Karnak sections, some in ruins, some still standing; on the west bank, the mortuary buildings of the land of the dead.

The complex at Luxor is the first of these reached by the Nile in its northward course. From the river's bank to a point three hundred yards inland rise walls and heavy pylons sacred to the Theban triad of Amen, his wife Mut, and their son Khonsu. Like so many of the memorable structures in and around Thebes, the great temple of Amen at Luxor was begun by Amenhotep III (called Memnon by the Greeks) who reigned from 1411 to 1375 B.C. Two enormous seated statues of Amenhotep III, carved in monolithic pieces of quartz that were carried upstream four hundred and thirty-five miles and are generally known as the Colossi of Memnon, are all that now remain above ground of his funerary temple. His temple to Amen, on the other hand, was not only preserved but extended by his successors. Not even the heresy of the King's son Amenhotep IV — who changed his name to Ikhnaton, embraced Aton as sole god, and deserted Thebes for a new capital at Ikhetaton — ended the older city's growth.

The famous clustered papyrus columns that form the forecourt of the temple at Luxor were dedicated in Amenhotep III's lifetime. His successors — including Tutankhamen, Harmhab (a general who became Pharaoh), and Ramses II — added fourteen enormous columns, a pylon, three of six colossi, and a pair of obelisks (one of which now graces the Place de la Concorde in Paris). Most of these embellishments were the work of Ramses II (1292-1225 B.C.), busiest of Egypt's builders, who also decorated the temple's walls with scenes of his victories over the Syrians and Hittites. In later ages other races and religious sects also wrought their changes in the temple. Alexander the Great restored its sanctuary, where he is shown in *relief-en-creux,* wearing the double crown of Upper and Lower Egypt and holding with Horus the symbolic key of life. The Romans built their own shrines there, generations of Christians raised churches on the site, and today a Moslem mosque occupies the temple's western end.

Grand as it is, the temple at Luxor serves only as a prelude to the majesty of Karnak. The entire site of the temple of Khonsu at Karnak — covering sixty-two acres — is surrounded by a brick wall seventy-eight hundred feet long. At its center stands the temple of Amen, sometimes said to be the most imposing religious complex of all antiquity. Though a building may have existed there in the Old Kingdom, the surviving construction was started by Amenemhet I at the beginning of the Twelfth Dynasty. Amenhotep I (c. 1557 B.C.) built a new temple at right angles to the old one, thus enlarging the over-all structure. The great temple was further added to by succeeding kings — including Amenhotep III — down to the time of the Ptolemies.

Six pylons, erected by several Pharaohs, lead to the temple's hypostyle hall, the largest single chamber of any temple in the world (it is about three-quarters the size of Notre Dame in Paris). Down the center of the hall there are two rows of columns sixty-nine feet high, with avenues of smaller columns forty-two feet high on each side. The roof is composed of enormous slabs of stone. In the dimness of this forest of stone gleam colored inscriptions that trace the temple's history, give praise to the gods, and record the royal stories of its various builders.

Between two of the massive pylons soars the tallest obelisk in Egypt, placed there around 1485 B.C. by Queen Hatshepsut. The daughter of Thutmose I by his principal queen Ahmes, this curious woman, who seems to have been a mixture of Borgia and Tudor, married her half brother Thutmose II. Her husband named as his successor a son by his concubine Isis, so on her husband's death Queen Hatshepsut first assumed the regency and later seized the throne, masquerading as a man and even wearing a false beard. The boy she had supplanted later succeeded her as Thutmose III and at once began to despoil her monuments. However, he spared the greatest of these, the unique funerary temple that Hatshepsut had begun at Deir el-Bahri, on the west bank of the Nile near Thebes. Nestling in a bay of a huge cliff, it is approached by three graceful terraces connected by a ramp that leads through great porticoes to a sanctuary cut deep into the rock. The temple is adorned with figures of Horus and the jackal-headed god Anubis, a lord of the lands of the dead.

At Thebes, paradoxically, the domain of Anubis is cut off from the city proper by the life-providing Nile. The bodies of the Pharaohs, their queens, and their lieutenants were ferried across the river in state to exist through eternity. Never was mortality more deified than in the religion of ancient Egypt. As the descendants of the gods, the Pharaohs thoroughly believed that their bodies would survive, and at various points during royal funerary rites the priests would stress this physical indestructability. "Thy bones perish not," they used to intone, "thy flesh sickens not, thy members are not distant from thee." Legend attributes the discovery of embalming to Anubis, who was supposed to have first used it on the body of Osiris. In fact, the practice probably dates from about the Fifth Dynasty (2750-2625 B.C.) and reached its highest development around 1000 B.C., the time of the Twenty-first and Twenty-second Dynasties.

When a Pharaoh died, his body was carried to a tent or pavilion, where the embalmers first drew out the viscera through an incision in the left side. The heart was left *in situ,* but the brain was removed. The cavity was washed and the body placed up to its neck in a solution of salt or natron. After several weeks, by which time the skin had peeled off and the other fatty deposits had dissolved, the body was washed and desiccated. (The viscera were once sealed in four vases of alabaster called canopic jars, but a later practice was to replace them in the body.) The torso and skull were then packed either with linen or with sand and mud, and the body was anointed with a mixture of resin and fat. Finally, it was wrapped with resin-soaked bandages. Then began the elaborate burial ceremonies known as "Opening the Mouth," by which the mummy was supposed magically to recover the use of its senses. The Egyptians believed that the incense and libations employed in the services would restore warmth and the life fluids to the mummified corpse.

Thus fortified against decay, the Pharaoh's body was taken to a tomb that was expected to protect it through the ages while his soul journeyed westward. Such tombs, built to be impregnable to the ravages of time, form the necropolis of Thebes. In death as in life, the distinctions of rank are observed: kings lie together, their queens at some distance, and beyond them the nobility. The custom began with Thutmose I, whose body was the first to be buried in the Valley of the Kings, near Luxor. It is a place of silence where neither bird nor insect can be heard. Robbers have ransacked most of the tombs there, but the contents of a few — notably that of Tutankhamen (c. 1358 B.C.) — have survived, hidden for centuries by rock falls or drifts of sand.

Only when the archaeologists Howard Carter and Lord Carnarvon uncovered Tutankhamen's tomb in 1922 was the splendor of a Pharaoh's pomp in death revealed to the modern world. Tutankhamen's mummy wore a mask of gold on its head and shoulders, and lay in a solid-gold coffin. The latter, in turn, was placed in two outer coffins of gold-covered wood, one of which still remains inside the stone sarcophagus, on whose lid is carved the Pharaoh's likeness. The decoration of the burial-chamber — delicate yet ornate in design — is generally naturalistic, following the fashion set by Tutankhamen's father-in-law, the heretic Ikhnaton.

The tombs in the Theban necropolis — Tutankhamen's is an example — were intended only for the reception and protection of the sarcophagi. Basically, the tombs consisted of a number of connected chambers cut deep in the rock, although sometimes the cliff face at the entrance was quarried away to form an open platform or courtyard. Some Pharaohs were also commemorated by mortuary temples; such buildings, however, were erected behind the high cliffs between which the Valley of the Kings lies. The temple of Ramses III (1198-1167 B.C.) at Medinet Habu is the best-preserved of those built during the New Kingdom. Together with the earlier temples of Seti I and Ramses II, it demonstrates that during the Nineteenth and Twentieth Dynasties the Pharaohs' mortuary temples were patterned increasingly on the shrines across the river that were dedicated to the gods. Each had the same arrangement of courts, pylons, hypostyle halls, and sanctuaries.

The architecture and the carvings of Ramses III's temple belong to an art that in the Pharaoh's time was already in decline; the artistic vigor of the Eighteenth Dynasty is lacking. In addition, the Coptics — early Christians — damaged the temple's Osiris columns while building a church in a courtyard, and Coptic houses still surmount its walls. Here, as elsewhere among the relics of Egyptian antiquity, time and the actions of men have changed the face of the past. The thousand-ton colossus of Ramses II, probably the largest single stone ever quarried, and described by Diodorus in 60 B.C. as "without flaw or blemish," has fallen to the Theban sand. In the reign of Ramses IX, toward the end of the Twentieth Dynasty, the tombs of Seti I and Ramses II were robbed — as others had been before them — and the Pharaohs' mummies were burned.

Meanwhile, as the worldly power of the princes of Thebes began to wane, that of the priests of Amen grew. The Nile in its course no longer reflected the march of armies bound for conquest but mirrored instead the solemn rites of an increasingly influential but nevertheless equally doomed theocracy.

Plates

173

The great temple of Amen at Karnak. At left is a newly placed colossus of Ramses II; the obelisk in the center is sixty-four feet high.　　[1961]

174-175

Ptolemaic portal before the temple of Khonsu at Karnak. In the foreground are the remains of one of the ram-headed sphinxes that once lined the road from the Nile.　　[1947]

175

Granite pillars in the Hall of Records at Karnak display reliefs typical of the Eighteenth Dynasty.　　[1947]

176-177

Top: The temple of Amen at Karnak. The ruined wall beside the entrance to the hypostyle hall on the left has since been restored, and a second colossus — shown on page 173 — faces the one shown here.　　[1947]

Bottom: The temple of Amen at Luxor, begun by Amenhotep III. The fourteen enormous columns at the right were completed by his successors.　　[1961]

178

Roman sanctuary in the forecourt of the temple of Amen. The columns have Corinthian capitals.　　[1947]

179
Hollow relief of Alexander the Great (*right*) with the god Horus on the wall of the sanctuary in the temple of Amen at Luxor.   [1961]

180
Merneptah, son of Ramses II, carved in pink granite on the lid of his sarcophagus at Thebes.   [1947]

181
The outermost of the three coffins of Tutankhamen at Thebes, with his carved and gilded likeness on the lid.   [1947]

182-183
The vaulted ceiling of the burial chamber in the tomb of Ramses VI at Thebes.   [1947]

184
One of four mourning goddesses depicted in Tutankhamen's gold shrine at Thebes.   [1961]

185
Mummy mask of Tutankhamen, of solid gold inlaid with glass and semiprecious stones. Surrounding it are jewelry and other objects from Tutankhamen's tomb.   [1947]

186
Wall painting from the tomb of Queen Nefertari at Thebes. The goddess Hathor and the falcon-headed god Harkhte welcome the queen to the nether world.   [1947]

186-187
The burial chamber of Ramses VI at Thebes. On the column at the right is the Pharaoh holding the goddess of truth in his hand.   [1947]

188
The inlaid gold back rest of Tutankhamen's throne, now in the Cairo Museum, showing a queen applying unguent to the young Pharaoh's body.   [1961]

189
A painted box from Tutankhamen's tomb pictures

the Pharaoh in a chariot battling the Assyrians (*top*) and the Africans (*bottom*).   [1961]

190
A bas-relief of two princesses, part of a procession carved on the walls of the tomb of Kheruef at Thebes.   [1947]

191
An unfinished tomb decoration at Thebes shows Seti I (*right*) making an offering to the god Osiris.   [1947]

192
Colossi of Memnon (Amenhotep III) at Thebes.   [1947]

193
Polygonal columns in the portico of Queen Hatshepsut's funerary temple at Deir el-Bahri. [1961]

194-195
Queen Hatshepsut's temple, one of Egypt's architectural masterpieces, seen from the Nile. *Below, right:* A portrait statue of the queen found at Deir el-Bahri, now in the Metropolitan Museum of Art, New York.   [Both 1961]

196-197
Mortuary temple of Ramses III at Medinet Habu. Columns lining the second court (*right foreground*) bear partly destroyed figures of Osiris.   [1947]

198-199
The huge fallen colossus of Ramses II, in the Ramasseum at Thebes.   [1947]

199
A seated colossus of Ramses II in the temple of Amen at Luxor, photographed (*top*) in 1947 and (*bottom*) again in 1961. In the interim, the Egyptian Department of Antiquities has restored several parts of the face, and completely removed the sand from the torso.

200
Moonlight on the famous colonnade of Amenhotep III in the temple of Amen at Luxor. [1947]

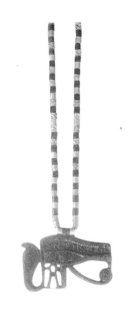

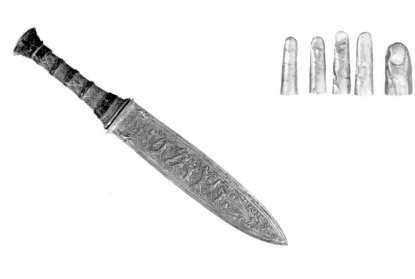

IX
The Sun God

When Amenhotep IV — an extreme individualist and Egypt's first monotheist — succeeded his father on the throne in 1375 B.C., he attempted a complete reform in his people's religious observances. Prior to his reign, the ram-headed god Amen had been the chief Theban deity, often identified with the sun god Ra. Below Amen-Ra a complex of lesser deities presided over the living and the dead in an awesome and confused thearchy. All this Amenhotep IV swept away, demolishing the old gods and stripping the Nile of its divinity, replacing the whole concept with a new one: that of a single god, Aton. Amenhotep IV's efforts had a vast effect on the theology, the political and social power structure, and the art that were the legacies of his predecessors.

Soon after Amenhotep IV's succession to the throne, he changed his name (which meant "Amen is satisfied") to Ikhnaton (Aton is satisfied). He introduced his new faith to Thebes by building a temple to Aton at Karnak and by erasing the name of Amen from all the Theban monuments, not even sparing his father's memorials (although evidence that he was devoted to his father remains). Even the word "gods" in the plural was expunged. In the preceding century, however, the warrior king Thutmose III had helped to develop an Egyptian national priesthood by joining all the temples in the country under a High Priest of Amen. The newly unified and already propertied priests were given title to much of the conquered land in Asia. To say the least, they were reluctant to relinquish power, property, or prestige when Ikhnaton began to press his reforms. The task of trying to do so in Thebes against the stubborn and determined opposition of the established priesthood finally forced the Pharaoh to a decision: to found a new capital city.

Ikhnaton selected a site, where today Tell el 'Amarna stands, half way down the Nile between Thebes and the sea. It was then a barren plain, a part of the Arabian Desert shut in by low hills east of the Nile. He named the city Ikhetaton (Horizon of Aton) and, like his followers, referred to it as "the seat of truth." The city's boundaries were marked by stelae on which prayers and official precepts were incised. On one that is still standing the inscription reads: "It [the site] had belonged to no god or goddess, also not to any lord or any mistress, and no other person has the right to tread upon it as the owner." The city, five miles long, was laid out parallel to the Nile, its three main avenues intersected at right angles by smaller streets. Its buildings were of sun-dried brick, and all were unusually commodious, even those of the common laborers. Ikhetaton contained at least four sanctuaries sacred to Aton. Eastward, in the low cliffs outside the city, lie the tombs of Ikhnaton's nobles that have yielded to archaeologists most of the writings — in effect, hymns of praise to Aton — that reveal Ikhnaton's then-radical religious beliefs.

It may even be that Ikhnaton intended to establish his monotheistic religion throughout the world he knew. Under his aegis, one city similar to Ikhetaton was built in Nubia and another in the conquered lands of Asia. Indeed, Ikhnaton's concept was not only of a sole god whose spirit was everywhere but of one whose universality must be acknowledged. Thus the following hymn, as rendered by J. H. Breasted:

> Thou makest the Nile in the Nether World,
> Thou bringest it as thou desirest,
> To preserve alive the people.
> For thou hast made them for thyself,
> The lord of them all, resting among them;
> Thou lord of every land, who risest for them,
> Thou sun of day, great in majesty.
> All the distant countries,
> Thou makest also their life.
> Thou hast set a Nile in the sky;
> When it falleth for them,
> It maketh waves upon the mountains,
> Like the great green sea,
> Watering their fields in their towns . . .

The Nile's inundations were attributed by the followers of the new sect to natural forces controlled by Aton, whose High Priest the Pharaoh had now become — guarded, meanwhile, by his Nubian and Asiatic mercenaries.

For fifteen years, preoccupied with God, Ikhnaton remained in the city he had built. Hundreds of clay tablets bearing cuneiform writing testify to his correspondence on both religious and secular subjects with his tributaries and allies outside Egypt. But his absorption in religion damaged his political power. After a revolt in Syria that heralded the decay of Ikhnaton's empire, the court moved back to Thebes — whether just before or just after the Pharaoh died, archaeologists are not sure. No trace of Ikhnaton's mummy or of that of his beautiful wife Nefertiti remains. All the reforms of the king known as the "Religious Revolutionary" came to naught, for the priesthood at Thebes at once reinstated Amen and his appendant gods. The great city-state soon sank back into its old beliefs and resumed its drift toward oblivion.

Flowing past Thebes, the Nile enters what might be termed Middle Egypt, although technically the river region is divided into Lower Egypt (the Nile Delta), Upper Egypt (the Nile valley below the Delta region), and various governorates for Cairo, Alexandria, and Damietta. The river in Middle Egypt is about half a mile wide and looks like liquid sand. The only color of any brightness to be seen in the area is the green along its banks, which are narrow on the east but wider on the west. Passing the Temple of Hathor in ancient Dendera, the Nile comes to a barrage at Nag Hamadi, west of Qena. The purpose of this barrage, like that of others along the Nile's course, is to raise the level of the river so that some of its waters will flow into canals without the use of pumps. By such means, more farmland is produced, and the towns scattered along the riverside gradually become larger and more prosperous.

Typical of such towns is Abu Tig, on the west bank of the river south of Asyût. Like the houses that were built at Ikhetaton centuries earlier, most of those in Abu Tig today are of sun-dried brick composed of mud from the river, water, and straw. The walls are whitewashed when the construction has been completed. Considering the climate, the resulting structures are fairly strong; it is fortunate that the rainfall is too low to dissolve the primitive materials of which the houses are built. The occupants of these adobe-like homes are usually farmers and their families pursuing a way of life little changed since the days of their ancestors. Most of them are afflicted by the curse of the Nile, bilharziasis — that terribly debilitating disease which the river carries all the way from Lake Albert. Along this section of the Nile the principal crops — almost all of them concentrated on the west bank — are wheat, clover, garlic, beans, onions, and other assorted vegetables, although increasing emphasis is being placed on the cultivation of sugar cane. Above these green acres rustle the fronds of date palms. Today, as in ancient times, dates are a staple food, not only for their nutritional value and flavor but also because when dried in the desert heat they can long be kept without spoiling.

The same heat and desert dryness have done much to preserve the relics of the Egyptian past. But not even the climate has sufficed to keep them all in perfect condition. Time and nature have taken their toll, for example, on the thirty-nine tombs in the limestone cliffs of Beni Hasan that overlook the river seventy-five miles north of Asyût. The fine art work in the tombs is gradually being deformed by excrescences growing out of the walls; in fact, some of the more famous paintings, done in the Twelfth Dynasty, can now barely be seen. Just the same, more than enough remains here, as it does elsewhere in the country, to reveal a great deal about the techniques of the long-dead Egyptian painters. Three kinds of surface were generally used for murals. The most primitive was a mud and straw mixture like that still used to face the walls of Egyptian houses; it was sometimes overlaid with a plaster containing powdered stone. The second type of surface consisted of a coat of stucco; the third, of smoothed limestone. The painter first affixed guide lines soaked in red paint; when plucked, they left straight lines across the wall. He then drew in his outlines, laid the background in, completed the painting's details, and finally reinforced the outlines, usually in red. His pigments were all derived from natural substances which were powdered and added to a solution of gum in water; in most of the color schemes simple earth colors predominate: the red, brown, and yellow ochers. From copper the painter got his blues and greens; from soot, his black. His brushes were sticks or reeds hammered at one end to separate the fibers. There were sometimes minor variations in technique, but these were generally the means the ancient Egyptians employed in decorating free-standing sculpture and bas-reliefs as well as in creating murals.

Bas-reliefs like those in the temple of Seti I (1313-1292 B.C.) at Abydos, a hundred miles northwest of Thebes, were first carved into hard limestone; color was then added. The work in Seti I's temple is considered among the best in Egypt, although it does not belong to a period particularly noted for its artistic achievement. The bas-reliefs decorate the second hypostyle hall, which contains no fewer than seven sanctuaries. In one of the latter, a mural depicts Seti I receiving the mace and curved sword of majesty from Amen-Ra. The temple's first hypostyle hall, a hundred and seventy-one feet long and thirty-six feet wide, contains a notable avenue of heavy columns and a number of bas-reliefs featuring Seti II's son and successor, Ramses II. Ramses' creative fervor so overcame his filial piety that he was prompted to have his father's image chiseled from the walls and his own carved thereon. In its day, Abydos was also a place of great funerary importance, for it was here that the decapitated body of Osiris was supposedly interred. The mummies of many rulers were carried to Abydos by boat, and it was the practice to raise commemorative tablets to the Pharaohs there.

Models of the Pharaohs' funerary boats have been found in a number of tombs and probably present a reasonably accurate picture of those vessels. The tomb of Meket-Ra in Thebes, for instance, contained a superb group of boats, each intended for a different purpose (one for traveling, another for use as a floating kitchen, and a third for fowling), as well as a series of paintings of domestic scenes that have thrown light on the everyday life of the times that existed some two thousand years before Christ. Among the other interesting evidence from the past discovered in some of the tombs is proof that the early custom of burying the Pharaohs' followers with them was later superseded by a more humane practice: carved statues or murals — representations of the retainers — took the place of the real people. The tomb of Mesehti at Asyût is an example. It yielded an impressive company of Nubian archers fourteen inches high, beautifully carved in wood and painted.

In those ancient days, when an Egyptian monarch numbered his minions in the hundreds of thousands, the proud vessels of his court must have swept in majesty along the whole navigable course of the river, whether bearing the Pharaoh in his living person or in the pomp of death. The royal barges are long gone. Yet the trading feluccas of today are sailed south before the prevailing winds, and rowed north with the help of the Nile's unchanging current, just as were those barges of the Pharaohs scores of centuries ago.

Plates

207

The east bank of the Nile at Qena, fifty miles downstream from Luxor. A water buffalo and a donkey have come here to drink, and feluccas — loaded with earthenware pots — to trade. [1947]

208-209

Two views of the temple of Hathor at Dendera, near Qena, built during the Ptolemaic period. The Greeks of that time identified Hathor, the Egyptian goddess of love and joy, with their own Aphrodite. The cornice above the elaborate columns is Roman, with a Greek inscription, and the reliefs inside depict such figures as Nero, Caligula, and Cleopatra. [1947]

210

Bas-reliefs, considered among the finest in Egypt, in the temple of Seti I at Abydos, a hundred miles downstream from Thebes. The figures of three goddesses, Isis, Amentet, and Nephthys, shown at the side of Osiris (*extreme right*), have been carved lovingly into the very hard limestone. [1947]

211

An avenue of heavy columns in the first hypostyle hall of the temple of Seti I. Most of the reliefs in this hall are portraits of Ramses II, the son of Seti. [1947]

212

A relief of the dark-skinned Seti I kneeling before the gods Amen-Ra (*right*) and Harkhte in his mortuary temple at Abydos. This room is one of seven sanctuaries on the south wall of the second hypostyle hall. [1947]

213

A hollow relief of the same gods, Amen-Ra and Harkhte, this time with Seti's son Ramses II (*center*) wearing the double crown of Egypt, in a newer part of the same temple. [1947]

214

A holiday crowd filling one of the narrow streets of Abu Tig, a small village on the Nile south of Asyût, about midway between Aswan and Cairo. Abu Tig is typical of the many towns lining the river in so-called "Middle Egypt." [1947]

215

Women sitting before a wall painting on a white-washed house near El Minya, 150 miles south of Cairo. This elaborate depiction of the owner's pilgrimage to Mecca even shows the steamboat (*upper right*) on which he traveled. [1961]

216

Portrait bust (now in Berlin) of Queen Nefertiti, wife of Ikhnaton. About life-size, the bust was found at Ikhetaton in 1912 by a German archaeological team and has since become the very symbol of Pharaonic Egypt. [1952]

217

Colossal head of Ikhnaton, part of a full-length figure over thirteen feet high, now in the Cairo Museum. In its crossed hands the figure once held the flail and scepter that were the symbols of authority. [1961]

218

Ikhnaton, followed by Nefertiti and one of their daughters, making an offering to Aton, the sun god. This limestone relief, excavated at Ikhetaton and now in the Cairo Museum, suggests the tremendous change Ikhnaton's influence wrought in Egyptian art, transforming the idealized figures of previous dynasties into the naturalistic and even distorted forms seen here. [1961]

219

Two views of the ruins of Ikhnaton's palace at Ikhetaton, not far from El Minya. The capital city of Egypt from 1369 to 1358 B.C., Ikhetaton is now a deserted waste. [1961]

220-221

A company of Nubian archers, wooden figures fourteen inches high that date from the Tenth Dynasty, taken from a tomb at Asyût and now in the Cairo Museum. These figures were buried with their master, the Pharaoh Mesehti, in the hope that their originals too would have ever-lasting life. [1961]

222-223

The tombs at Beni Hasan, near El Minya over-looking the Nile. *Top:* Several of the thirty-nine tombs dug into the cliffs where nobles of the surrounding province were buried. *Bottom:* One of the fine wall paintings from inside the tombs: a wrestling match, with many holds identical to those used today, done in the manner of a slow-motion movie. [Both 1961]

224

A camel rider and his spare mount pause beneath date palm trees in an area of relatively extensive cultivation near Beni Hasan, to look back over the banks of the Nile. [1961]

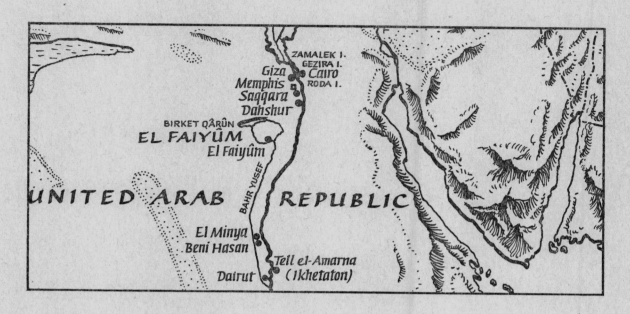

X

The Pyramid Builders

Past the barrage — 2691 feet wide — at Asyût, the Nile reaches Dairut and appears to split. The Nile proper continues north. Off from it to the west, but then turning north and paralleling the Nile, runs the Bahr Yusef, a once-dry bed of the old river that now carries water by the most important irrigation canal in Egypt — the Ibrihamiya — to one of the country's most fertile areas, the 770 square miles called El Faiyûm. This rich tract, not more than seventy miles southwest of Cairo, is the easternmost oasis in the Libyan Desert. In it lies Birket Qârûn, a shallow body of water occupying part of the basin of ancient Lake Moeris, around which a crocodile cult flourished in Herodotus's day. He recorded the local custom: "Those who dwell . . . about Lake Moeris consider them [crocodiles] to be very sacred; and they each of them train up a crocodile, which is taught to be quite tame; and they put crystal and gold earrings into their ears, and bracelets on their forepaws; and they give them appointed and sacred food, and treat them as well as possible while alive and when dead they embalm them, and bury them in sacred vaults." The crocodile cult was a minor one, however. Much, much more than crocodiles was buried — or was memorialized — in the area. For soon after the Nile passes Birket Qârûn it begins to enter another fabled land of the dead, marked by what are probably the most familiar monuments in the world and are certainly among the most interesting: the pyramids.

Now a hundred and seventy-five miles or so beyond Dairut, the Nile approaches Memphis, first capital of a united Egypt and older even than Thebes. Memphis is flanked north and south by the pyramid-tombs of kings. Some eighty such pyramidal structures have been found in Egypt, but most of them are by now mere heaps of rubble. Pyramid-type tombs were built over a period of thousands of years, from shortly after the beginning of the Old Kingdom (c. 3400 B.C.) to the end of the Ptolemaic Dynasty (30 B.C.), but the age of the true pyramid ran from the Third Dynasty to the

Sixth, and the art of pyramid-building reached its highest point in the Fourth Dynasty (2900-2750 B.C.). Halfway between El Faiyûm and Memphis, at Dahshur, stands the first pyramid that can be seen from the river on its way north.

Named the Bent Pyramid, because on its upper half its sides are more gently inclined than they are below, it measures 617 feet square at the base and rises 325 feet. It was built by King Snefru, whose reign flourished about 2920 B.C. at the end of the Third Dynasty. Also in Dahshur, and probably built by Snefru, too, is the earliest known tomb designed and constructed as a true pyramid: the Northern Stone Pyramid. A third pyramid nearby at Meidûm may have been built or completed by the same king; like all these buildings, it is a step pyramid.

A step pyramid may be said to be the second stage in the evolution of the true pyramid. The first stage was the mastaba, originally merely a sepulchral structure built above ground — long, low and flat-topped, with inward-sloping sides of brick or stone. As the mastabas became more elaborate, a shaft leading down to a deep subterranean burial chamber was added. The later mastabas normally consisted of three parts: an outer chamber for offerings, a secret inner chamber for statues of the dead, and an underground chamber for the sarcophagus. The early kings of Memphis and many of their followers were interred in such tombs at Saqqara, the necropolis of Memphis. Two kings built enormous mastabas at Abydos; one of these rulers passed into obscurity, but the other — the Pharaoh Zoser, probable founder of the Third Dynasty — had immortality thrust upon him by a member of his court, a counselor called Imhotep. The counselor eventually acquired greater fame than his king. He was vizier, scribe, priest, and — above all — physician and architect. Later, in Ptolemaic times, he was deified by the Egyptians as the god of medicine and was identified by the Greeks with Asclepius, the god of healing.

Imhotep constructed a vast building for Zoser at Saqqara, then added two similar but smaller structures on that base, achieving a roughly pyramidal shape. The end result, Zoser's Step Pyramid, measures 411 feet by 358 feet at the base and stands 204 feet high. Beneath it, tunneled into a rock and reached by a shaft a hundred feet deep, is a complex of corridors and rooms, including a burial chamber lined with red granite from Aswan. Zoser's Pyramid, like most of the others, is the center of a cluster of buildings. Pyramids were usually constructed on comparatively high ground, with a mortuary temple, enclosed by walls, nearby. A second temple often stood at the end of a sloping causeway where a canal leading from the Nile terminated. The buildings around Zoser's Pyramid are paneled with fine white limestone; Imhotep was the first to use stone on the grand scale. His example was followed by later pyramid-builders, particularly the Pharaoh Khufu (c. 2900-2877 B.C.), sometimes known as Cheops, whose Great Pyramid at Giza has long been known as one of the Seven Wonders of the Ancient World.

Khufu's monument is the largest pyramid ever built as well as the oldest of the three true pyramids at Giza that almost every tourist in Egypt visits. The three — often called the Pyramids, with a capital "P" — stand in a rocky landscape on a plateau a few miles southwest of Cairo. The Great Pyramid covers nearly thirteen acres. Its four faces, each forming an almost perfect equilateral triangle, are oriented to the four main points of the compass. The base measurements of the pyramid's sides do not vary from each other by more than eight inches; the stripping of the outer stones from the sides, each of which was originally approximately 755 feet long, has somewhat reduced their length. The pyramid is composed of 2,300,000 blocks of limestone weighing on average two and a half tons apiece (some weigh fifteen tons) and measuring as much as twenty feet by six feet. The joining of the blocks is so precise that it could hardly be equaled with modern tools. The interior construction, now exposed, is of limestone from the Mokkatam Hills near Cairo, but the outer covering — long since dragged away to fill the housing needs of Giza and Cairo — was of a finer grade of limestone. When it was finally completed, the pyramid was just over 481 feet high; it is now lower by thirty-one feet, due to the removal of the facing stone.

Herodotus records that the stone was brought up to the plateau from the river by a causeway that itself took ten years to build and that the construction of the pyramid took another twenty years.

All in all, he estimates, the completion of the project required the efforts of a hundred thousand men working steadily over a period of thirty years. Since Egyptian engineers used leverage and brute strength, but not pulleys, their method must have been to haul the blocks up long approach ramps which were built up higher with earth and bricks as each successive tier was constructed; the ramps were presumably dug away when the pyramid was completed. The entrance to the Great Pyramid is on the north side, some fifty-five feet above ground level. From it, a narrow corridor first leads down and then slants up to the rooms within the masonry (there is also a passageway to a chamber in the native rock below the monument). The main rooms include, in the order in which they are approached, the Queen's Chamber, the Great Hall or Grand Gallery, and — finally — the King's Chamber. The last room, which was supposed to be Khufu's permanent resting place, is roofed and lined with polished granite, but it is empty now, save for a lidless sarcophagus. Not even the herculean labors of his slaves or the master craftsmanship of his architects and engineers could guard Khufu from the desecrations wrought by men of later generations.

Greed and time have worked ravages on the Great Pyramid. When is was newly built it must have shone smooth and white in the bright sun of the desert; now, with its interior masonry exposed, it looks weatherbeaten and roughly textured. Among the thousands of other innocents who have ventured abroad and into Egypt, Mark Twain once climbed its slopes. This is how he described the experience: "Each step being full as high as a dinner-table; there being very, very many of the steps; an Arab having hold of each of our arms and springing upward from step to step and snatching us with them, forcing us to lift our feet as high as our breasts every time, and do it rapidly and keep it up till we were ready to faint, who shall say it is not a lively, exhilarating, lacerating, muscle-straining, bone-wrenching, and perfectly excruciating and exhausting pastime, climbing the Pyramids?"

The pyramid built by Khafre (or Chephren), Khufu's son and successor, stands nearby. It is 471 feet high and thus the second tallest pyramid. Built around 2850 B.C., it was originally cased in limestone and granite. A portrait statue of Khafre that was discovered in 1853 by Auguste Mariette (who was Egypt's first foreign-born director of governmental excavations and founded the Cairo Museum) is esteemed as one of the finest examples of three-dimensional Egyptian sculpture extant. A little larger than life-size and carved in hard gray-green diorite, it is a *ka,* a kind of icon representing the dead monarch. Its purpose was to guard the mummy while the soul of Khafre was absent, or even to receive that soul on its return should the dead flesh fail. During the burial rites prevalent at the time, the ka was accorded the same resuscitative attention as the mummy, including the ceremonial "Opening of the Mouth."

There are two more world-famous monuments at Giza. One is the third of the three Great Pyramids, which was built by the Pharaoh Menkure about 2800 B.C. Less than half as tall as Khufu's or Khafre's, it is considered by some to be the most perfect, although the original plan of coating it all in red granite was never carried out. The other magnificent monument at Giza is that historic enigma, the Great Sphinx. Khafre probably built it, but the drifting sands covered its entire 189-foot length until a later Pharaoh, Thutmose IV, was inspired by a dream — according to legend — to dig them away. The first modern excavations around the Sphinx, undertaken in 1818, revealed that it had been carved from a natural limestone outcrop and then supplemented by masonry. During the years it had been damaged by the vandalic gunfire of the Mameluke sultans, who ruled Egypt between 1250 and 1517. By 1925 the sands had again accumulated on the Sphinx and again were cleared away. But no one has yet convincingly explained the full symbolism of this human head (a woman's or a man's?) on a lion's body, recumbent in Giza, a place of royal interment.

Giza and Saqqara, up river from Memphis, together formed the great city's necropolis. Once a more important place even than Thebes, Memphis was for centuries both a religious and mercantile center and Egypt's capital. But it was razed and all its temples and splendors destroyed on the orders of Theodosius the Great (346?-395), Roman Emperor of the East. Later, its fallen stones were carried off by Arab invaders to build a new city — now known as Cairo — ten miles to the north, where the great river nears the end of its 4160-mile journey to the sea.

Plates

229

Portrait statue of Khafre, builder of the second highest pyramid at Giza. This *ka,* or icon, portrays the Pharaoh with a hawk, symbol of the god Horus, behind his head.   [1961]

230-231

The Bent Pyramid at Dahshur, built by Snefru, father of Khufu. *Top left:* Workmen hauling debris from the upper chamber of the pyramid, in a search for a still-unrifled burial room. *Bottom:* Clearing stone from this chamber.   [1947] *Right:* View through the date palm trees shows the peculiar shape of the pyramid.   [1961]

232-233

Third-century portraits, now in the Cairo Museum, found in the cemetery at El Faiyûm, about seventy miles southwest of Cairo. The paintings, done on wooden panels attached to their subjects' coffins, are Greek in style.   [Both 1961]

234

Farmers lifting water from the Nile by means of a shaduf into fields in the Faiyûm district. [1961]

235

The sphinx at Memphis, with the face of Amenhotep II. Twenty-six feet long and fourteen feet high, weighing some eighty tons, the alabaster figure stands alone in an area desecrated first by Theodosius and later by the Arabs.   [1961]

236-237

A canal on the ancient site of Memphis, reflecting the animals of pastoral Egypt — camels, water buffalo, and a donkey — with a line of date palms on the horizon.   [1961]

238

The desolate and barren desert to the east of Memphis, typical of the vast stretches in Egypt that are unnurtured by the Nile.   [1961]

239

A Bedouin mother and child at a camp in the Arabian Desert, east of the Nile. The Bedouins still camp in tents as they search the desert for grasslands for their camels and sheep.   [1961]

240-241

The step pyramid of Zoser at Memphis, with a number of other, later pyramids at left.   [1961]

242-243

Architecture surrounding Zoser's step pyramid. *Top left:* Restored protective wall, thirty feet high. *Bottom left:* Massive three-quarter columns in the hall of pillars leading to a tomb at the far end. [Both 1959] *Right:* The outline of the pyramid can be seen behind columns, once part of Zoser's funerary temple.   [1961]

244

One side of the Great Pyramid of Khufu at Giza, near Cairo.   [1947]

245

The two largest Pyramids at Giza; the first light of sunrise is reflected from the tomb of Khufu, left, to that of his son Khafre, right.   [1947]

246-247

The mysterious Great Sphinx at Giza, with the Pyramid of Khafre at left behind it and that of Khufu, right.   [1947]

248

Portrait statue of Nofret, a member of the court of Snefru who was buried near that Pharaoh's pyramid at Dahshûr; this ka is now in the Cairo Museum.   [1947]

249

Seated figure known as the Scribe. This famous limestone statue, only twenty-one inches high, was discovered at Saqqara, the necropolis of Memphis, and is now in the Louvre.   [1947]

250-251

The tomb of Ptah-Erouk, a minor official of the Fifth Dynasty, at Saqqara. The single low-ceilinged room (*right*) is lined with high-relief sculptures of Ptah-Erouk, his wife, and two sons. Above the figures a low-relief frieze (*left*) depicts the ritual slaughtering of cattle.   [Both 1947]

252

A wall decoration from the Fifth Dynasty tomb of the architect Ti, at Saqqara. The walls are almost completely covered with these finely carved low reliefs showing the daily life Ti hoped to enjoy again in the next world.   [1947]

247

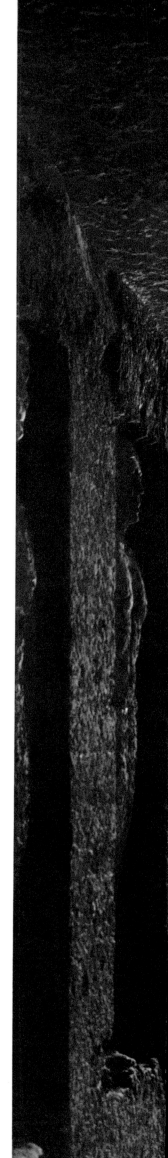

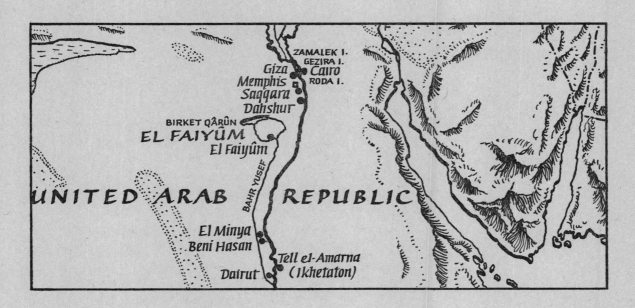

XI
Cairo
and Islam

Seen from the river at night, Cairo is a necklace of jeweled lights. By day it is a jumble of white building blocks animated by the activity of the biggest and most cosmopolitan population of any city in Africa. It is crammed with the polygenetic architecture that has resulted from a thousand years of mixing, adapting, and taking liberties with Arabian and European styles. It might be said that while Mecca is the spiritual heart of Islam, Cairo is its brain. In the mosques and universities of Cairo the theology and culture of the Moslems have traditionally been rejuvenated, and out of Cairo today comes a large part of the proselytizing zeal that seems to be spreading the Moslem creed increasingly through the awakening continent of Africa. When Cairo was founded on the Nile's banks the power of Thebes and Memphis had long passed. The history of Cairo is in a sense the history of modern Egypt.

The first settlement near the site of present-day Cairo was called Babylon by the Greeks and Romans who invaded it in the centuries immediately preceding and succeeding the time of Christ. It lay on the east bank of the Nile opposite the pyramids at Giza. In 614 A.D., the Romans used it as a camp for their legions and tried to defend it against an Islamic army sent from Baghdad by the Caliph Omar (581?-644). The Romans were overwhelmed by the Moslems, and Egypt passed from the West to the East. At first under the control of the Ommiads, who were headquartered in Damascus, it eventually (in 750) became part of the new Baghdad-centered empire of the Abbassides, a Moslem dynasty claiming descent from Mohammed's uncle. Shiite and Persian in origin, the Abbassides had extended the influence of Islam from the field of religion into that of temporal power. Amr ibn-al-As, the general who drove out the Romans, ruled Egypt under orders from the Ommiad caliphs, propagated the faith, and began to build the city that is now Cairo. His successors, both Ommiad and Abbasside, extended the city northward. One of them, Ahmed ibn-Tulun, gained his independence from Baghdad and is commemorated by one of the city's earliest "pure" mosques, in which no Roman or Byzantine influence is evident. The structure is still a graceful Cairo landmark.

The next invasion of Egypt came from the west. It was led by Jauhar al-Rumi, a general dispatched by the Fatimids — another Moslem dynasty, this one said to be descended from Fatima, daughter of Mohammed — who wished to shift the seat of their government eastward out of North Africa to the more desirable valley of the great river. In 969 Jauhar inflicted a decisive defeat on al-Fustât (then the name of what is now known as Old Cairo), took over the reins of power, and began adding on to the city, calling the resulting metropolis-to-be al Qahirah, or Cairo, "the victorious." A year later he founded Cairo's most famous mosque, El Azhar, in thanksgiving to Allah. It has been a center of Islamic learning ever since. Jauhar's masters moved to Cairo, made it their capital in 973, and ruled there for two hundred years, building ten great mosques and a number of palaces. Their dominion was terminated in 1171 after a series of campaigns waged against them by the armies of Nureddin, ruler of Syria. Soon after Nureddin's death a few years later, a thrusting young soldier in those armies took over control of Egypt and founded his own dynasty, the Ayyubids. His name was Saladin.

It was a time when Islam was menaced by a religion no less militant: Christianity. European Christians were on the march to recover the Holy Land from Moslem control. Using stone from the Pyramids, Saladin fortified Cairo against the Crusaders by raising a citadel, which still stands in the shadow of the Mokattam Hills. Having extended his empire into Yemen, Palestine, and Syria, he defeated the Crusaders in 1187 and captured Jerusalem. Saladin's descendants, divided among themselves and under repeated attack, managed to preserve the Ayyubid Dynasty for about a century. Ironically, they were overthrown in 1250 by the Mamelukes, mercenaries who over the years had been recruited as boys in Georgia and the Caucasus by both the Fatimids and the Ayyubids, converted to Islam, and trained in Egypt in the arts of war. The Mamelukes were savage, efficient, and aloof.

By the middle of the fifteenth century a rift had opened between the two halves of Islam represented by the Ottoman sultanate and that of Egypt. A war between the two powers resulted in the absorption of Egypt into the Ottoman Empire in 1517, when Cairo fell to the Turks. Despite the establishment in Egypt of a *pasha* (governor) responsible to the Ottoman Turks, the real power was shortly retrieved by the aggressive Mameluke beys.

For two and a half centuries feuds between Cairo and Constantinople flared desultorily, but when Napoleon's forty thousand troops sailed into Abukir Bay in 1798 — the first infidels to do so since the Crusaders — the rulers of Egypt were still Mamelukes. Cairo was held in dual sway by two of their beys, Ibrahim and Murad. The latter heard of the French invasion with disdain and rode off with three thousand or so of his cavalry to drive them into the sea. In July of 1798, Murad Bey was routed at Jibbrish. Still confident, he gathered his main force at Embaba on the west bank of the Nile, with the Pyramids in the background. He and Ibrahim Bey had mustered at least thirty thousand men, a third of them cavalry. There the medieval army waited, while Napoleon's well-equipped forces tramped upstream. Nine days later the Egyptians saw the French squares moving against them in the dawn across the desert floor. The Egyptians — bright in their silken turbans and chain mail, their scimitars whistling as they charged — hurled themselves upon Napoleon's veteran infantry. Within minutes most of the beys' men lay shattered at the cannons' mouths or torn apart by the measured volleys of the French divisions. But so bitterly did the Mameluke army strive, so ferocious was its valor, that the French took no more than a thousand prisoners. Murad and a few other survivors fled up river into Nubia. Brave as they were, as warriors the Mamelukes had been proved anachronisms.

Settled in Cairo in a palatial house commandeered from a Mameluke bey, Napoleon began to impose a rule of reason on Egypt. The intellectuals he had brought with him formed *L'Institut de l'Egypte*. The country's past was to be explored, her antiquities catalogued, her resources measured. Napoleon bridged the Nile with pontoons and planned a series of dams across it. He proposed to cut a canal at Suez, wore Egyptian clothes, and professed admiration for the Moslem faith. He applied logic to Egypt's multitudinous administrative problems and pressure on her taxpayers. But neither his rationalism nor his revolutionary ardor could win Egyptian adherence to his cause. Inured to conquerors, the Egyptians saw Napoleon as more oppressive than the Mamelukes. He meddled in more affairs and, worst of all, did so efficiently. Nor did such *bêtises* as stabling horses in the Azhar mosque endear the French to their reluctant hosts.

When the French quit Egypt late in 1801, expelled by the British and Turks, who in turn soon retired from the scene, the main legacy left by the foreigners was a political vacuum. It was filled by the adventurer who later ended the power of the Fung kings in the Sudan: Mehemet Ali. He had entered Egypt as the mercenary captain of a small band of Albanian brigands; he died there the founder of a royal dynasty. At once devious and brutish, far-sighted and ambitious, Mehemet Ali shaped Egypt into an independent state. He annihilated the power of the Mamelukes by the simple expedient of professing friendship for them, luring them to the citadel at Cairo, and massacring them there. He captured Mecca in a devastating campaign, and conquered the eastern Sudan. He turned back a British attempt at invasion and swept victoriously through Greece and Syria. At home he ruled with equal ferocity, reducing the *fellahin* to unspeakable poverty and his subject peoples to slavery. But his public works, like the great barrage north of Cairo, put Egypt on the road to prosperity. When Mehemet Ali died in 1849, Egypt was free of debt.

The fourth of Mehemet Ali's line, Said Pasha, incurred the first portion of the national debt that was to plague Egypt through the nineteenth century and well into the twentieth. Work on the Suez Canal was begun in 1859 during his reign. Under Ismail Pasha, Khedive of Egypt from 1863 to 1879, the cost of constructing the canal (which was opened in 1869), ineffectual wars in the Sudan and Ethiopia, archaic administrative practices, and a profligate court enlarged Egypt's debt. As a result, Ismail Pasha was forced to sell his shares in the Suez Canal to Great Britain. When Ismail Pasha's son and successor, Tewfik Pasha, agreed to joint British and French control over his nation's finances, riots ensued, and the British intervened. By 1882 Egypt had, to all intents and purposes, become a British protectorate. And by early in the new century the British had gained control of the Nile from its sources to the sea.

In 1936 — more than half a century after they had taken over in Egypt — the British began to withdraw from the country. King Farouk, last of Mehemet Ali's dynasty, was seventeen years old at the time. But the British withdrawal was not fully effective until 1954, two years after the ousting of Farouk in a military coup. In 1956 Colonel Nasser, who had initiated the revolution from behind the scenes, abolished the parliamentary system, had himself elected President of a one-party Egyptian Republic, and began an attempt to assert his leadership of the Arab world. To that end, he engineered a union between Egypt and Syria under the name of the United Arab Republic. Nasser was named its President. Although Syria has moved in and out of the union, the U.A.R. remains the official name of the Egyptian state, and a politically unified Arab world apparently remains Nasser's long-range aim.

Even the most cursory glance shows that Cairo is a city heavy with the weight of centuries of Arab taste. Within its confines exists one of the richest concentrations of Moslem art and architecture in the world. The tombs of the Mamelukes, desolate but still ornate, are clustered together on Cairo's southern edge. Four hundred mosques are scattered throughout the city, the finest of them being the one that Sultan Hasan built between 1356 and 1359. Its minaret measures 270 feet from ground to pinnacle and is thus the highest in Cairo. Hasan's mosque is nearly six hundred years older than its neighbor, the mosque called El Rifai, whose inhabitants are dervishes so expert at putting themselves into a trance of spiritual exaltation that they become quite indifferent to the physical pain of having nails driven through their cheeks, chewing glass, or swallowing fire.

Although Egypt's constitution proclaims the nation an Islamic Arab state, Islam is not the only religion observed in Cairo. The great Ben Ezra Synagogue in the old part of the city was built nine centuries ago and is still in active use. Despite the recurring clashes with Israel, more than 13,500 Jews are said to remain in Egypt. The Copts, however, are by far the largest religious minority in the country. There are 1,100,000 throughout Egypt. The direct descendants of those ancient Egyptians to whom the Romans brought Christianity, they have held fast to their Christian faith ever since the first Moslem invasion.

Cairo's population numbers more than 2,500,000 and is growing. The encouragement of new industries has spawned housing developments in the suburbs; in the center of the city, blocks of multiple apartment buildings, angular and functional, rise beside the minarets and domes. Houseboats crowd the Nile along the pleasant islands of Gezira and Roda, at whose southern tip stands the Nilometer, placed there in 716 A.D. to measure the river's rise and fall. Over all of Cairo, five times a day, floats the clear warbling cry of the muezzin — the Mohammedan crier of the hour of prayer — summoning the faithful. It is a sound that has been heard in Cairo for more than a thousand years. If the missionary zeal of Islam continues, it may eventually be heard over the length of the Nile from the Mediterranean to the heart of Africa.

THE RULERS OF EGYPT IN TRANSITION

(All dates A.D. after that indicating start of Roman control)

Roman Emperors	30 B.C.-640 A.D.
(During this period Egypt was part of the Roman Empire. It was conquered by Moslem armies from the Middle East in 640.)	
Ommiad Dynasty	646-750
Abbaside Dynasty	750-969
Fatimid Dynasty	969-1171
Ayyubid Dynasty	1171-1250
Saladin	1171-1193
The Mameluke Beys	1250-1517
Ottoman Emperors	1517-1798
(During this period Egypt was officially part of the Ottoman Empire, but the Mamelukes gradually regained the real reins of power.)	
Napoleon Bonaparte	1798-1801
(During this period Egypt was officially part of the Ottoman effective control of the country despite the disastrous sinking of his fleet by Nelson in Abukir Bay soon after the French invasion. When Napoleon left, a period of political vacuum ensued.)	

THE RULERS OF MODERN EGYPT

VICEROYS (KHEDIVES) *

Mehemet Ali	1805-1848
Ibrahim Pasha	1848
Abbas I	1848-1854
Said Pasha	1854-1863
Ismail Pasha	1863-1879
Tewfik Pasha	1879-1892
Abbas II	1892-1914

SULTANS

Hussein Kamil	1914-1917
Ahmed Fuad Pasha	1917-1922

KINGS

Fuad	1922-1936
Farouk	1936-1952

(After the ousting of Farouk in a military coup in July 1952, his son was named nominal ruler under a regency council. But on June 18, 1953, the crown was abolished and Egypt was declared a republic.)

PRESIDENTS

Mohammed Naguib	1953-1956
Gamal Abdel Nasser	1956-

(Since his proclamation of the United Arab Republic in 1958, Colonel Nasser has served as President of both Egypt and the U.A.R.)

* The title of khedive was granted the rulers of Egypt, still nominally part of the Ottoman Empire, by the Sultan Abdul-Aziz in 1867, in recognition of Egypt's growing independence. But Mehemet Ali had long since in effect founded his own dynasty, which lasted until the abdication of Farouk in 1952.

Plates

259

A view over Cairo of the Nile and the three Great Pyramids of Giza, looking southwest from the Mokattam Hills. The ancient mud-brick houses and domed mosques of one of the older sections are seen in the foreground, with the multistory hotels and modern factories of the downtown section on the near (eastern) bank of the river. [1961]

260-261

Cairo's Liberation Square, so named to commemorate the 1952 revolution, filled with holiday crowds. The picture was taken from the Nile-Hilton Hotel, which stands between the square and the river. The buildings in the background are typical of the architecture of central Cairo. [1962]

262

Top: The ruined mosque of El Khalamati on the lower slopes of the Mokattam Hills, near the ancient burial ground known as the City of the Dead. The mosque still has the domed mausoleum and a tall minaret from which the Moslem *muezzin* cries the hour of prayer. [1959]

263

Top: The Sultan Hasan Mosque has the highest minaret in the city; built in 1356-59, it is considered by many to be the finest mosque in Egypt. The small minaret to the right of the dome was added at a much later date, after the original spire collapsed during an earthquake. The mosque across the street is El Rafai, center of an order of dervishes. The haze in the background is caused by the *khamsin* winds, which blow in from the desert in the early spring. [1947]

262-263

Bottom: The interior of the Mehemet Ali Mosque,

Cairo's most recent, designed by a Greek architect in the nineteenth century. The interior walls and the four ornate square columns that support the ceiling of this room are of alabaster, giving the building its popular name of the Alabaster Mosque. [1959]

264

Courtyard of the "Hanging Church" of the Copts in Cairo. The elaborate ornamentation is typical of Coptic architecture. The Copts, whose Christianity has survived under Moslem rule for 1300 years, are "true" Egyptians, not Arabs, and their religious services are still conducted partly in the language of Egypt of the third century A.D. [1961]

265

Interior of the Ben Ezra Synagogue, built some 900 years ago in one of the oldest parts of Cairo, and still used by the city's sizable Jewish community. In the place of honor, below the arch in the center of the photograph, is the ark of the covenant. [1959]

266

Top: Houseboats on the canal surrounding Zamalek Island in the Nile near Cairo. Many such boats are moored on the river, most of them rather ordinary two-family structures, but some of them quite solid and luxurious. [1947]
Bottom: A view of the Nile looking eastward from a building on Liberation Square, showing one of the newer sections of Cairo. The spire at the right is a communications tower completed in 1961. At the far left, poking just above the horizon, are the Great Pyramids of Giza. The Tahrir Bridge in the left foreground is one of several over the Nile in the vicinity of Cairo. [1962]

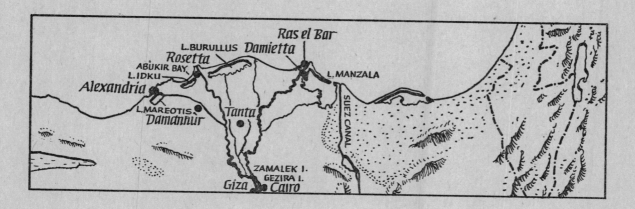

XII
The Fertile
Delta

Seven miles downstream from Cairo the Nile begins to spread out across a vast delta, its waters meandering through rich and fertile soil for almost 150 miles before they finally reach the Mediterranean. Although it was once allowed to split up in its own haphazard way, taking seven separate routes to the sea, the river is now confined to two main channels, the Rosetta branch (146 miles long) flowing to the northwest and the Damietta branch (151 miles long) flowing to the northeast. From these two channels the Nile's water is sent through thousands of little irrigation canals that criss-cross the Delta, bringing water to an area of some 8500 square miles and making the region one of the most fertile and intensely cultivated areas on the earth.

If Egypt is dependent on the Nile, it is even more vitally dependent on the Nile Delta. For here is the nucleus of the country's agriculture and hence the core of its wealth; agriculture from this single area makes up more than sixty per cent of Egypt's total exports, and without its abundant crops — chiefly cotton — Egypt today would be a land rich only in history. Some eleven million people — forty per cent of the total population — are crowded into this area, with densities up to an amazing sixteen thousand people per square mile (compared with Washington, D.C., which averages twelve thousand people per square mile).

Nature has been mixed in its blessings to the Delta. The average temperature is a fine fifty-two degrees, but from March to May a hot, sandy wind called the *khamsin* blows in from the desert at speeds of up to ninety miles an hour, raising the temperature as much as thirty-five degrees in two hours and spreading a thick haze across the region. The alluvial soil carried down from the Ethiopian highlands to form the topsoil (at the enormous rate of about fifty-six and a half million tons a year) is rich in iron oxide and alumina, which is perfect for a number of cereal crops; but the soil is also high in salt content, and only such salt-resistant plants as cotton and corn grow well in it without fertilization. During flood time there is enough water for excellent irrigation, but during the rest of the year the Nile diminishes, and the meager rainfall, averaging four and six tenths inches per year, is insufficient for most crops. In fact, during Pharaonic times the Delta was not extensively cultivated and was used chiefly for growing fruits and wine grapes.

But what nature overlooked, man has supplied, and the result is that the Delta is now Egypt's cornucopia. In the early nineteenth century the far-sighted Mehemet Ali realized that the Delta would have enormous potential as a cotton-growing region if only the annual floods could be checked, and regular instead of periodic irrigation established. He therefore ordered the construction of two low stone dams more than fifteen hundred feet long across the Rosetta and Damietta branches of the Nile, which caused the water to back up into reservoirs that could be drawn upon for regular irrigation. Completion of these dams, or barrages, meant that for the first time the Delta could grow three crops a year instead of just one, could have water during the normally dry months from December to August, and could host crops like cotton that resist heat only when well-irrigated.

Mehemet Ali's original barrages were completed in 1861 and finally reinforced and heightened in 1890; four more barrages have been constructed since. Today the range of Delta crops is vast, including cotton, corn, rice, barley, wheat, onions, clover, alfalfa, sugar cane, peanuts, sesame, millet, flax, beans, oranges, tangerines, lemons, and dates. The Delta is now largely responsible for the production of Egypt's field crops, which brought more than one billion dollars into the nation's coffers in 1961.

In the Delta, as in the rest of cultivated Egypt, cotton is king. Known to the Pharaohs only in its tree form, cotton as a shrubby plant has been in Egypt for just a century and a half, but it is a safe generalization to say that today just about every Egyptian farmer grows as much cotton as he possibly can, for upon this most of his cash income depends. Currently some eighteen hundred thousand acres are under cotton, and each acre has an average yield of 438 pounds — about a hundred pounds more than an average U.S. acre. Cotton production has jumped from 319,000 metric tons in 1953 to 479,000 metric tons in 1961, and income from cotton has spiraled from $277,000,000 in 1956 to $418,000,000 in 1961. Egyptian cotton is recognized to be the finest cotton in the world, for the conditions of the Nile Delta produce a cotton ball with fibers up to one and three fourths inches long, a full three fourths of an inch longer than the best U.S. cotton. This "long-staple" cotton is especially valuable in cloth manufacturing and commands the highest prices on the world market. Egypt today is the world's number one producer of cotton in terms of quality and the fifth largest producer in terms of quantity (after the U.S., China, Russia, and India).

From the air, the Delta seems to be a collection of rectangles, as the long, straight irrigation canals cut at right angles across farms throughout the region; each rectangle seems to have its own distinctive color, ranging from the dark brown of a newly plowed field through the soft white of a ripe cotton farm to the solid green of a clover patch. Very little disturbs the regularity of the scene; only the carefully planted trees — date palms, sycamores, poplars, acacias — and a few rocky outcrops break the flat surface. On the edges of the Delta, however, the rocky deserts rise in jagged cliffs from the basin (the Libyan Desert on the west, the Nubian Desert on the east), and at the Delta's northernmost fringe a series of salt marshes and small lakes break up the smoothness. These lakes, breeding grounds for a number of disease-bearing insects, are formed as the Nile drops its heavy loads of silt, and the Delta thus pushes steadily into the sea. The four largest lakes are Lake Mareotis, on the fringes of Alexandria in the west; Lake Idku, near the Rosetta branch to Alexandria's east; Lake Burullus, between the arms of the two Nile branches; and Lake Manzala, between Damietta and the Suez Canal in the east.

Most of those living on this flat and fertile terrain are *fellahin,* the hearty farmers who make up the majority of the Egyptian population. These people, direct descendants of the farmers who worked for the ancient Pharaohs, still retain the same quiet strength and dignity that their ancestors show in pyramid paintings. They are slightly above medium height (averaging five feet nine inches), with pale brown skin and often small tattoo marks, the signs of some ancient and surviving cult, on their foreheads, chins, and temples; males past middle age usually wear a beard as a symbol of dignity. The fellahin's dress is drab compared with that of sub-Saharan Africa but extremely practical for the high temperatures and strong, dusty winds. The men wear wide cotton pants with a draw-string belt, a loose shirt, and — over everything — a *gallabiya,* a wide-sleeved, collarless shirt that falls to the ankles; on their heads they usually wear a brown felt skullcap called a *lebda,* and on their feet calf or sheepskin slippers, if anything. The women also wear cotton pants, underneath a long dress which trails on the ground, and in public they wrap themselves in a *milaya,* a long black cloak they use to cover their heads and faces in the Moslem tradition; the somberness of this costume is lightened by colorful necklaces and bracelets and, for married women, copper or silver anklets. The children wear a loose-flowing, striped cotton dress similar to pajamas.

A fellah's hut is usually made of Delta alluvium, which is extremely hard and resistant when dry, over a frame of date-palm lumber. The flat roof, also made of alluvium, is used for storage of grains and food and is connected to the ground by a simple outside staircase or ladder. Inside, the rooms are generally bare except for a few mats for sleeping and sitting, some cooking pots, and perhaps a low table; there are no windows, but air enters through small vents high up on the walls. Most houses have a small inside courtyard used for stabling such valuable domestic animals as donkeys and water buffalo.

A fellah's farm is usually no bigger than an acre, and many fellahin do not have even this much; in Egypt as a whole more than two million people own less than an acre, only 600,000 have from one to five acres, and a mere 154,000 (one half of one per cent of the population) have more than five acres. Because his plot is so small, the fellah often is forced to work for larger landowners, although the present government is trying to divide up the larger holdings so that every farmer can have a share. On his farm the fellah depends on simple tools — wooden plows, hand hoes, sickles, tree trunks for rollers — and sturdy animals like the ass (which is indigenous to Egypt), the buffalo, and the ox.

Though often small, the Delta farms are nevertheless productive. Each farmer grows at least three different crops: in the winter (November-May) wheat for his family and clover or alfalfa for his animals; in the summer (May-August) cotton or rice for cash; and during flood time (August-November) corn and beans for his family. The difficulty with this system is, of course, that it puts a severe burden even on the Delta's rich soil, and fertilizers, domestic and imported, are essential to reinvigorate the earth; but the fertilizer (or insecticide) used for one crop may prove harmful to the others that grow in the same spot. As part of its agricultural reform the government has experimented with community farming, whereby large areas planted with a single crop can be "rested" with alfalfa during the off-seasons and the use of fertilizer is thus made unnecessary, but so far this communal scheme has not found much favor with the individualistic fellahin.

The children of the fellahin are of special concern to the Egyptian Government, which hopes to give them far better education and training than their parents — more than fifty per cent of whom are illiterate — have had. Expanding its education budget from $15,700,000 in 1940-41 to $155,400,000 in 1961-62, the government has concentrated on technical and agricultural training schools to build up a core of men receptive to modern farming methods and capable of improving the country's industrial production. At the same time it is building new primary schools at the rate of some four hundred a year and has made education for children between the ages of six and twelve both free and theoretically compulsory; unfortunately, however, only half of this age group actually attends school, for many parents feel that their children are more useful on the farm, picking cotton or driving a buffalo around a water wheel, than if they simply knew how to read and write.

The present government is also concentrating on the fellahin themselves, and as part of its agrarian reform program it has confiscated 1,650,000 acres from large landholders and, as we have seen, has distributed about 500,000 of them to landless peasants; another 300,000 acres will be redistributed in the next five years. In the Delta itself the government embarked in 1953 on an ambitious experiment in land reclamation, trying to turn the desert area south of Alexandria into a prosperous farming area known as Liberation Province. It linked the region to the Rosetta branch of the Nile with the new Tahrir canal, laid out several new and well-planned towns, and gave land to some 22,000 fellahin and their families. In 1958 Egypt was forced to cut back on its program, partly because of bad weather and unexpected diseases and partly because the bureaucratic effort of relocating so many people proved overly cumbersome, but there are several thousand families in the province today who own and successfully farm their own land.

But though the fellahin are the backbone of the Delta, they are not the only inhabitants. The townspeople — traders, merchants, exporters, etc. — are also crucial to the area, and many of Egypt's largest cities are located there: Alexandria, with 1,500,000 inhabitants, is the country's second largest city; Tanta, between the two Nile branches, is the fifth largest; Damanhûr, near the Rosetta branch, is the ninth largest; and Zagazig, near the Damietta branch, is the tenth in size. Each of them has more than 125,000 people, and all are bustling, colorful combinations of contrasts: winding dirt roads and long paved avenues, crowded bazaars and modern shops, fellahin in ragged gallabiyas and businessmen in Western suits. A side street in a town like Tanta is always exciting, with horse-drawn carriages (still the usual means of transportation) rolling by, peddlers hawking from the side of the road, small traders in shacks and tents, donkeys with market loads on their backs, men standing in knots arguing politics or farming, women carrying jugs on their heads, children out to scavenge or beg, and over it all is the faint haze of dust raised from the unpaved street.

The two towns at the very tip of the Nile's channels also have this bustling spirit to them. Damietta, at the head of the Damietta branch to the east, has become a key city for small manufacturing, especially of low-quality cloth for the lower and middle classes (cloth manufacturing is currently Egypt's largest industry). In an attempt to diversify its economy away from its dependence on agriculture, the government today is trying to build up small industries. In 1961 it launched a five-year industrialization scheme with $1,200,000,000-worth of investment, and it plans to increase industrial output from the current $1,400,000,000-worth to $1,700,000,000 by 1966. Throughout the Delta, cities and towns like Damietta are joining in this industrial growth, and plans are now under way for expanded factories in cloth manufacturing, cottonseed-oil processing, cement production, and even iron and steel manufacturing.

Rosetta, at the head of the Rosetta branch to the west, is also a busy town with expanding industries, but its most interesting sight is not a modern factory but the ruins of a fortress — Fort St. Julien, four miles north of the city. It was at this fort that a French engineering officer in 1799 came upon a small, three-and-a-half-foot-long slab of black basalt covered with strange inscriptions which turned out to be the decisive key to the understanding of Egyptian history. The slab was the famous Rosetta Stone, and the inscriptions were in Greek and in hieroglyphic (sacred) and demotic (common) characters. Comparing the known Greek with the unknown hieroglyphics, Jean François Champollion in 1822 finally succeeded in deciphering the characters, thus paving the way for later scholars to read the pyramid hieroglyphics and to reconstruct the language of Pharaonic Egypt. The slab itself was probably created originally in honor of Ptolemy Epiphanes, a second century B.C. ruler of Alexandria.

Like Damietta and Rosetta, Alexandria, on the westernmost fringe of the Delta, is a bustling city, by far the most modern as well as the largest city of the region. It stands against the Mediterranean, some twenty miles west of Rosetta, and its main street runs for several miles parallel to the water, affording the modern villas and offices at its edge a consistently beautiful seascape. A town of only four thousand people in the early nineteenth century, Alexandria boomed as a seaport when cotton became Egypt's biggest export, and today it is the third largest port on the Mediterranean (after Marseilles and Genoa). Because of its vast commercial activities, it has become a thoroughly cosmopolitan city, with Greeks, Levantines, Israelis, Italians, and Frenchmen forming more than ten per cent of its population and with a wider variety of restaurants than probably any other city in Africa. Oddly enough, Alexandria was until 1950 the only city in Egypt with a fully constituted municipality; then Cairo got around to making itself legally a city.

Alexandria is, of course, rich in history. Founded in 322 B.C. by Alexander the Great after his conquest of Egypt and laid out in efficient rectangles by Alexander's architect Dinocrates, it quickly became an important center of Greek culture and at one time had a famous library of more than four hundred thousand documents. First under the rule of the Ptolemy family and then — from the first century B.C. — under the Romans, it was developed into the most vital commercial city on the European-Indian trade route and was the official capital of Egypt for nearly a thousand years. Around the third century A.D. it began to decline in stature as Egypt sank into chaos, and for the next fifteen hundred years it suffered under a succession of rulers — Arabs, Fatimids, Egyptians, Ottomans, and French. It was not until Mehemet Ali at the beginning of the nineteenth century started to turn Egypt into a modern trading nation that Alexandria regained its position as a major commercial center.

Alexandria's most interesting historical monument is a tall spire mistakenly called Pompey's Pillar. It actually has nothing to do with the Pompey family of Rome, but was erected in 302 B.C. by Publius, the Roman Prefect of Egypt, to commemorate the Emperor Diocletian's successful quelling of an Alexandrian revolt. Built on the highest spot in the city and almost ninety-nine feet high although only thirty inches around, the pillar is a commanding sight from anywhere in Alexandria.

But for all its richness — both historical and commercial — Alexandria would be nothing were it not for the fertile Delta and the Nile that brings it to life. Its people, no less than those of Burundi, Uganda, the Sudan, and Upper Egypt, must depend for their very lives upon the great, bountiful river.

For wherever it runs, the Nile dominates. And as it now pours out into the waiting Mediterranean after its mighty 4160-mile journey, the Nile still remains king, for in the Delta, as in the headwaters, *Aut Nilus, Aut Nihil* — either the Nile, or nothing.

Plates

273
Zeid Ali, a fellah or farmer, in the new Liberation Province of the western Delta region. This province was carved out of the desert by water from the Rosetta branch of the Nile as part of a land reclamation scheme under the Nasser government's agrarian reform program.   [1959]

274
Women planting rice shoots in a paddy near the Damietta branch in the Delta; bundles of seedlings can be seen in the water behind them. [1947]

275
Children, under the watchful eye of a foreman (with parasol), picking worms from cotton plants on one of the Delta's many cotton farms. The youngsters' size and nimble fingers make them ideal for the job.   [1947]

276-277
A typically busy street in the town of Tanta. Though automobiles, as seen at the far right, are increasingly popular, they have not replaced horse-drawn carriages like the one in the center of the photograph. The merchant in the stall on the right is selling baskets; in the foreground is a man hawking dolls.   [1959]

278-279
A children's fair at Damanhûr, near the Rosetta branch 38 miles southeast of Alexandria. The swings have small boxes — on which the children stand — rather than seats. Their frames are collapsible, so that they can be taken down and set up again in the next town.   [1961]

280
School children on a homemade swing at Rosetta, with the Delta's ubiquitous date palms in the background. The little boy is wearing the typical striped, loose-hanging pajamas.   [1961]

281
A woman of the Liberation Province carrying an earthenware water jar resting on a small circle of plaited straw. The water comes from the newly built Tahrir canal. Though a number of villages now have a community faucet, many women still carry six or seven gallons of water a day from the nearby canals.   [1959]

282-283
Women washing their brass cooking pots in the Tanta canal. The woman behind the stone wall wears a black *milaya* over her head; she is leading a water buffalo and following a milk cow, both animals vital to the fellahin.   [1959]

284-285
Top: Young boys fishing at the mouth of the Rosetta branch of the Nile, where it flows into the Mediterranean. The sea begins just beyond the line of palm trees in the upper right-hand corner. *Bottom right:* A water wheel (known as a *saqia*) raising water from one of the Delta's many canals. The large horizontal wheel turns another vertical wheel below it that dips small clay pots into the canal and empties them into narrow ditches leading to the fields.   [Both 1961]

286
The sphinx from Tanis, a town in the eastern Delta that was the "summer capital" of Egypt during the New Kingdom. Now in the Cairo Museum, this sphinx bears the face of Amenemhet III (c. 1849-1801 B.C.).   [1961]

287
A felucca on the Rosetta branch seen through the ruins of Fort St. Julien, just north of the town of Rosetta, where the famous Rosetta Stone was found in 1799.   [1961]

288
The Damietta branch of the Nile as it flows into the Mediterranean. This aerial photograph shows the village of Ras el Bar, on the outskirts of Damietta, on the right bank, and former British Army warehouses on the left.   [1947]

289
The so-called "Pompey's Pillar" and a sphinx in Alexandria. The column, polished red granite from Aswan, stands amid the ruins of the Serapeum, a temple built by the Ptolemies in the second century B.C., but was itself erected by the Romans, in 302 A.D.   [1959]

290
Moonrise over Alexandria, seen from the Mediterranean. The buildings, which front on an avenue running parallel to the sea, are in the eastern section of the city, in the district called Camp de Cesar. It was in Alexandria that the geographer Ptolemy drew the map of the great river whose source, he believed, was in the "Mountains of the Moon."   [1959]

(Page numbers in italics refer to photographs)

Abba Island, 83, 84

Abu Simbel, 119, 120, 122, *123, 124-25, 126-27*

Abu Sir, 102, *113*

Abu Tig, 203, 206, *214*

Abukir Bay, 254, 257

Abydos, 203, 205, *210, 212,* 226

Albert, Lake, 19, 20, 21, 22, 41, 42, 43, 44, 62, 121, 203

Albert Nile, 21, 41, 42, 44, *58-59,* 63

Albertine system, 20, 21

Alexandra, Mount, 22, *27*

Alexandria, 202, 268, 270, 271, 272, *289, 290*

Al-Fustât (Old Cairo), 254

Arabian Desert, 120, 147, 201, 228, *239*

Armant, 150, *163*

Aswan, 19, 99, 101, 102, 119, 120, 121, 122, *134, 135, 140,* 147, 148, 150, 206, 226, 272; Dam, 120, 122, *132*

Asyût, 203, 204, 206, 225

Atbara River, 19, 20, 85, 120, 121

Babylon, 253

Bagemder, 85

Bahr el Ghazal (River of the Gazelle), 42, 63

Bahr el Jebel (River of the Mountain), 42

Bahr el Zeraf (River of the Giraffe), 63

Bahr Yusef, 225

Baker, Mount, 20

Batn el Hagar (Belly of Rocks), 101, 102, *112-13*

Beni Hasan, 203, 206, *222-23*

Bigeh Island, 120, 122, 130-31

Birket Qârûm, 225

Black Lake, 22, *26*

Blue Nile (Bahr el Azraq), 19, 20, 85, 86, *93, 96, 97,* 100, 121

Bohen, 99

Bujubu Stream, 22

Burullus, Lake, 268

Burundi, 19, 21, 39, 42, 61, 271

Butiaba, 42

Cairo (al Qahirah), 20, 147, 202, 206, 225, 226, 227, 228, 253, 254, 255, 256, 258, *259, 260-61, 262-63, 264, 265, 266,* 267, 270

Camp de Cesar, 272, *290*

Cataracts, 99, 100, 101; First, 99, 119, 120, 122, *132, 142;* Second, 99, 99-100, 101, 102, *110, 112-13, 113,* 119; Third, 101; Fourth, 99; Sixth, 99, 102

Congo, 19, 20, 21

Congo system, 21

Cush, 100

Dahshur, 226, 228, *230-31*

Dairut, 225

Damamhûr, 270, 272, *278-79*

Damietta, 202, 268, 270, 272, *288;* Damietta branch of the Nile, 267, 268, 270, 272, *288*

Darfur, 83

Delta, 20, 100, 121, 202, 267, 268, 269, 270, 271, 272, *273, 274, 275, 280, 284-85,* 286; *see also* Egypt, Lower (Nile Delta)

Dendera, 202, 205, *208-209*

di Savoia, Mount, 20

Deir el-Bahri, 169, 172, *193*

Dweru Bay, 21

Edward, Lake, 20, 21, 22, *34, 36-37, 38,* 41

Egypt, 19, 20, 42, 64, 83, 85, 99, 100, 101, 102, 119, 120, 121, 122, 147, 148, 149, 150, 168, 172, 201, 202, 203, 205, 206, 225, 227, 228, *238,* 253, 254, 255, 256, 257, 258, 267, 268, 269, 270, 271, 272; Lower (Nile Delta), 119, 148, 168, 202, 267, 268; Middle, 202, 206, *214;* Upper, 119, 148, 168, 202, 271

El Faiyûm, 225, 226, 228, *232-33, 234*

El Jebelein, 86, *90, 91*

El Kab, 150, *158-59*

El Minya, 206

El Obeid, 83, 84

Elephantine Island, 121, 122, *136-37, 146*

Embaba, 254

Emin, Mount, 20

Equator, 20, 21

Equatoria, 84

Ethiopia, 19, 20, 63, 85, 100, 255, 267

Fashoda, *see* Kodok

Fazoghli, 100

Fort St. Julien, 270, 272, *287*

George, Lake, 20, 21

Gessi, Mount, 20

Gezira, 85, 86, *92,* 256

Giza, 226, 227, 228, *229, 244, 245, 246-47,* 253, 258, *259, 266*

Great Rift Valley, 21

Halfa Digheim, 102, *114*

Hierakonpolis, 150

High Dam, 101, 102, 119, 120, 121, 122, 148, 150

Ibrihamiya canal, 225

Idfu, 102, 148, 150, *154-55, 156-57*

Idku, Lake, 268

Ikhetaton (Tell el 'Amarna), 168, 201, 202, 206, *219*

Ishango Bluff, 22, *36-37*

Isna, 148, 150, *160-61*

Jibbrish, 254

Jonglei, 121

Juba, 63, 65

Kagera River, 20, *39*

Karissimbi, Mount, 21

Karnak, 167, 168, 171, *173, 174-75, 175, 176-77,* 201

Karuma Falls, 41

Kenya, 19, 40

Khartoum, 19, 61, 62, 63, 64, 83, 84, 85, 86, *96, 97,* 99, 100, 102; Khartoum North, 86, *96*

Khashm el Girba, 120, 121

Kodok (Fashoda), 63, 64, 66, *80-81*

Kokki, 102

Kom Ombo, 147, 148, 150, *151, 152-53;* valley, 121

Kordofan, 83, 86, 87, 100, 102

Kyoga, Lake, 20, 41, 43, *46-47,* 121

Levant, 167

Liberation Province, 270, 272, *273, 281*